GunDigest PRESENTS

THE SUPPRESSOR HANDBOOK

PATRICK SWEENEY

Published by

Gun Digest® Books, an imprint of Caribou Media
Gun Digest Media, P.O. Box 12219, Zephyr Cove, NV 89448
www.gundigest.com

To order books or other products call toll-free 1-800-258-0929
or visit us online at www.gundigeststore.com

CAUTION: Technical data presented here, particularly technical data on handloading and on firearms adjustment and alteration, inevitably reflects individual experience with particular equipment and components under specific circumstances the reader cannot duplicate exactly. Such data presentations therefore should be used for guidance only and with caution. Caribou Media accepts no responsibility for results obtained using these data.

Cover photo by Richard King

ISBN-13: 978-1-946267-22-1
ISBN-10: 1-946267-22-8

Designed by Dane Royer
Edited by Corrina Peterson

Printed in The United State of America

10 9 8 7 6 5 4 3 2 1

RELATED TITLES FROM GUN DIGEST

Gun Digest Book of Suppressors

Gun Digest Book of Tactical Weapons Assembly/Disassembly

Standard Catalog of Military Firearms

gundigeststore.com

CONTENTS

. . .

INTRODUCTION

...

Most firearms books focus on gear. Gear, tools, equipment – goodies – are a major focus for a simple reason: better tools usually give better results. This is something that the parents of music students are told, "If you want little Jimmy to do his best as an XYZ player, you need to buy a good one."

A suppressor is a large-ish investment in time and money. Don't abuse it, or you risk having your months and dollars busted, like this.

This is true up to a point. If little Jimmy has no chops, no skill at music, you can hand him a Stradivarius or Guarneri and he'll make a hash of the music. Too much does not deliver greater rewards. You want to get little Jimmy something good enough that he has a fair chance of succeeding, but not so expensive that it breaks the bank.

So, the question to answer is how much do you spend, to get how good an instrument, to make sure your skills are fully used.

What we'll do here is not a test and comparison of suppressors. The contents of this book simply provide background information to help you choose a suppressor. You can view it as your "I won't make a mistake in buying my suppressor" title, but let me offer a prediction: your first probably won't be your only.

In February 2016, the ATFE published a small and interesting bit of information: there were 900,000 registered suppressors in the U.S. By the time this book gets into your hands, that number could easily be over a million. That's a lot of previously forbidden items getting out in to the real world.

To give you an idea of the magnitude of that data point, there are just under 180,000 transferable machine guns in the U.S. The term "transferable" means those that you or I or any other lawful citizen can purchase. There are other machine guns, known as Dealer's Samples, that can only be bought and sold between dealers, and then only when they have a need for one, like buying it to demonstrate to a police department, for instance. There are all the R&D machine guns built by manufacturers, but those items cannot even be sold to other manufacturers. (We'll leave out of this the 12 million M16s and hundreds of thousands of belt-fed machine guns the government has bought, for they might as well be on the moon for as much chance as we'll ever have of seeing them, absent enlistment.)

The Hughes Amendment to the FOPA 1986 stopped sales of new machine guns (MGs). That's why, the last time I saw a transferable M16 (and not a NIB one at that), the price tag on it was $25,000. No, that's not a typo, twenty-five grand for a Stoner-system rifle with a giggle switch.

The reason is simple: Econ 101. Restrict the availability of a desired item and the price goes up. Transferable MG numbers were forever frozen, and the price just went up and up.

The good news was that suppressors were not also covered. I'm not sure suppressors were even known about in the anti-gun community in 1986, let alone being on their radar. So, they were left alone.

It took a while, and a bunch of states had to change their laws, but by the early 21st century suppressors became hot commodities. This was due in large part to two things: inflation and price increases in machine guns. When MG prices went to "You've got to be kidding me!" levels, those who wanted more than just a bolt-action deer rifle looked around,. They saw lots of ARs, but also suppressors.

The inflation part stems from the original law covering suppressors, the National Firearms Act of 1934, aka NFA or NFA 34. Not being able to ban firearms back then, the legislators did what they could – they taxed them. The transfer tax was set at $200 per, and thankfully not adjusted for inflation.

Suppressors come in a variety of sizes, for different calibers and uses. There is no "one size fits all," so don't expect one.

In 1934, $200 was a pile of cash. In fact, if you had a decent job then (not common, it was the Great Depression, after all) $200 was a lot of money. A quick check turns up some average annual incomes of the time: construction worker $907, registered nurse $936, steel worker $423, U.S. congressman $8,663. $200 was a bite for most people, and intended to be so, representing more than two months of income for that construction worker. The Congressman?

Not so much a problem, then and now.

I was on a recent trip, and over dinner one of the people in the tour made the kinda-shocked, sort-of amused observation that people change their behavior to adjust for taxes. Well, duh. That, for a lot of people, is the main reason to have a tax. And was meant entirely to be the reason for the transfer tax. It was meant to be a bar to purchase and to change behavior.

Fast-forward to the beginning of the 21st century and a $200 transfer tax is not big. Not exactly miniscule, but in an age of $1,000+ a year cell phone plans, a one-time $200 tax is not a big deal. Heck, at the price for a flavored latte plus tip for the barista at your local over-priced coffee emporium, $200 lasts as long as that construction worker had to work to earn it.

So people in the 21st bought suppressors and not machine guns.

A third reason making suppressors a hot commodity, but definitely not near the top, at least not in the beginning, is quiet for gun clubs. Convincing your local gun club to let you shoot your brand-new-to-you machine gun is going to be tough, if they aren't already doing it. While a suppressor is exotic (still, in some places) the decrease in noise is welcome at a lot of gun clubs, who are in a constant wrangle with the neighbors over noise. The machine gun represents an increase in noise, and a marked change in the nature of that noise. The sound of a machine gun is instantly identifiable. "Holy cow, Martha, they are shooting machine guns at the gun club. Call the police!" Suppressors? A good suppressor on a .30 rifle can make it sound like a .22LR to your neighbors. The smart ones will love it. the rest will still grumble.

Once you go quiet, you won't go back.

The fun of it is something it takes a lot of getting used to. Maybe you never do. The fun of seeing other club member's eyes light up when they realize what you've got, and the "Can I try it?" impulse never gets old.

In the course of this book, we'll go over some of the same material in several chapters, doing it from different directions or highlighting different considerations. This is a complex area of firearms (not that any of them are simple) and I want to make sure you have complete coverage.

And my prediction of the future? Yes, a lot of shooters will search for the "one suppressor to rule them all," but even after they've found it, they usually go back for more.

Buying requires information, research, and finding a place to buy. You can't just buy one over the counter at your hardware store, like they can in Finland.

There is much talk at the moment of the HPA, the Hearing Protection Act, which will (if/when passed) remove suppressors from the purview of the NFA and make them the equivalent of plain old firearms. We might find that, in the time between writing this and it getting to press, the HPA has passed, and a lot of the information is old hat. Also, the HPA will remove the $200 transfer tax from purchasing a suppressor.

Me, I'm a lot less sanguine. It will pass when the supposed adults in Washington find it to be in their interest to pass it, and not just because it's a good idea and we all desire it. (I know, there I go, being cynical again.) My advice: $200 is not that big a bite, don't pin your hopes and dreams on the HPA just to save two Benjamins. If you want one, buy one. If/when the HPA passes, there is built in (or the promise of same) refund for transfers for a certain amount of time before, perhaps six months.

If you buy a suppressor, pay the tax and the HPA passes, then you get your $200 back. If it has been longer than six months, well, just consider the $200 you paid as the price of getting your suppressor that much earlier.

Plus, there's an old adage that my father passed along as a lesson learned from the Great Depression and WWII: "Get yours before the hoarders all do." My prediction is that if/when the HPA passes, it will not take until lunch the next day for every single suppressor in inventory to be sold. There will be a million people calling stores or driving to gun shops, looking for the ten thousand suppressors on the shelves at that moment. It could come to pass, and you could then end up waiting six months just for the manufacturers to catch up with demand. So much for getting rid of the waiting time.

Remember the ammo shortages? How long did you wait for .22LR ammo?

Don't wait, don't wish, buy one now. Well, after you've read this book, anyway.

So, let's get to work. Or fun.

CHAPTER 1

WHY?

• • •

Once we get past the reflexive response of "Why not?" the situation becomes a bit more problematic. You see, this isn't a simple purchase. As we'll get into in the buying-specific section, purchasing a suppressor is not an impulse buy where you can slap down the plastic on a whim and walk out with a new goodie, at least not at the time of this writing.

So, we must have good reasons to jump through the hoops, if only for our own peace of mind, even if we don't have to justify the purchase to someone else, like husband, wife, whoever.

First is the lure of the forbidden. For a long time, suppressors were found only in the realm of Hollywood, where various assassins, spies, special agents, Special Ops troopers and others used them. The rest of us? Too bad, so sad, those toys aren't for you. Now, with almost every state allowing them, and suppressors being found on every range and gun club, they are no longer forbidden fruit, but still attractive.

Of course, the same legacy creates resistance. You can still go to gun clubs and find the old guard saying, "silencers are for assassins, we won't have them here." Which leads to the real reason to have suppressors: noise.

Noise is bad for your hearing, and while it would seem to be obvious, a lot of shooters still haven't gotten this memo. Oh, many will grudgingly stuff the little foam hearing-protection thingies into their ears, but they really don't take hearing protection seriously. They do it only because the range rules require it, and some might even make a production of reluctantly doing so. This attitude comes primarily from two areas: hunters and the military.

Hunters will tell you, with a straight face, two laughably ridiculous things. One, they must be able to hear their prey, because hearing is important. Like you are going to hear an elk at 250 yards, before he smells the coffee on your breath and the antiperspirant you put on that morning, or hears the muttered epithet you said through gritted teeth when you walked into the tree. Second, your ears "shut down" when you are hunting, and the tension you are under somehow protects your hearing.

At the risk of turning off my hunting readers who might be interested in this book and suppressors, I have to throw the B-S flag on both.

The animals you are hunting have better hearing than you do. And, their continued existence depends on their paying attention to anomalies in background noise. They'll hear you before you hear them. When I was a bow hunter, lo these many decades ago, I could ghost through the woods. I could sneak up on people and follow them for long periods of time. (It was entertaining, there and then, now it would just be creepy.) The deer? Not a chance. I'd have to be very lucky to "ghost" up on one of them. They would hear me every time. Staying still was the only way to remain unobserved. So, you aren't going to hear the deer, elk, moose, whatever, first, unless you are sitting down, not moving, and they are upwind.

Second, just because your brain registered the sound of the .30-06 as a "pop" doesn't mean you have negated the laws of physics. Brains aren't that powerful, and physics doesn't work like that. The compression wave of air that hit your eardrum hit it just as hard, regardless of your paying attention or not. There's no valve or flap inside the ear canal that closes to protect your hearing when you are under stress.

What does happen is your brain, under stress, has to categorize the torrent of information as to its relative importance. That there was a

It is in the nature of firearms to be noisy. Some situations are noisier than others, like this class of police officers with rifles. When the command to fire is given, you want to be wearing muffs over earplugs.

noise is important. Just how much importance the brain assigns to that noise determines how loud it seems to be, but that is not an accurate representation of how loud it actually is. Opinion does not trump reality.

I've mentioned this before, but I once did a survey of gun writers to see who had worn protection, how much, for how long, and how much hearing they had remaining. The answers were simple: the professional gun writers you read all expressed regret that they had not started protecting their hearing sooner and been more diligent, and all of them wished they could get back what they had lost.

Plus, they were a lot more optimistic about how much they still had. I mean, when a guy who says he still has 80% of his hearing has to lean across the dinner table to hear you, cupping a hand by his ear, he really doesn't have 80% left.

The military guys? The military insists on hearing protection, not based on any altruistic reason, but as a preemptive administrative move to beat back the potential rate of hearing loss disability claims once guys and gals who have served reach retirement age. But, the opinion of soldiers is that they have to skip protection because they need to hear what is going on around them or they might not survive.

The question I always have at this point is this: let's assume that the foamies take 20-25% of your current hearing away in the course of protecting you. This might be a problem in a combat environment, when you need to hear what is going on around the next corner, going house-to-house. What do you do when the same combat environment, after lots and lots of shooting, explosions and big engines, has taken 20-25% of your hearing, permanently? You are now where you'd have been at the start, but still with no protection and only more loss in your future.

The answer for a lot of shooters is to invest in electronic earmuffs. These use external microphones to hear, then small speakers inside to project the sounds to you. They have a built-in method of "clipping" or shutting off the noise to your ear, once it has reached 85 decibels. They used to cost $1,000 or more. The best still do, but the cheap ones (that work more than well enough for the majority of us) are now under a couple of hundred bucks.

Besides the personal aspect, there is the social. A firing line under a roof or indoors, where everyone is using a centerfire rifle, is an extremely noisy place. There, you'll want foamies in your ears and muffs over them, and it still won't be fun. If you've ever been on the line on a weekend before opening day of deer season, you know. Running a line of police officers for a patrol rifle class is also no treat. (I've done both, they are noisy beyond belief.)

This noise is a real hindrance for many gun clubs, who have found that suburbia has located and subsequently surrounded them. My own gun club went through that 25 years ago, and the problem for many clubs has only gotten worse. Adding suppressors keeps the noise down, and that is a good thing for gun clubs.

Noise is also a bad thing when you are trying to get new shooters to enjoy shooting. Assuming you aren't one of those moronic show-offs who hand a hard-kicking handgun or rifle to their girlfriend and say, "Go ahead, it's no big deal," you want new shooters to enjoy shooting. A suppressor takes the harshness out of the muzzle blast, which is a big part of the turn-off to new shooters. It also dampens felt recoil (although not as much as some suppressor advocates will tell you), and that also is a good thing.

Plus, if they haven't been keeping up on firearms changes, handing a new shooter a suppressed rifle or handgun and watching them shoot "a spy gun" is a hoot. They'll think so, too.

Noise is tiring. If you are camped out over a prairie dog town for a day's shooting, you'll see your success rate drift down through the

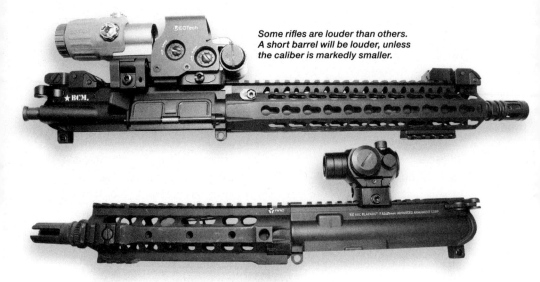

Some rifles are louder than others. A short barrel will be louder, unless the caliber is markedly smaller.

day. That's not just due to recoil and sun, but also noise.

And last, accuracy is a factor. The effect of a suppressor on accuracy is subtle, and it takes a full set of variables: an accurate rifle, accurate ammunition and a good shooter. That combo will punch smaller groups suppressed than when un-suppressed.

The subset of rifles known as short-barreled rifles, or SBRs, is particularly bad in the noise department. Putting a suppressor on a short rifle makes it a whole lot less work to shoot.

And finally, this is America. Everything that is not expressly forbidden is allowed, and when the only impediment is money and a little paperwork, it s almost your duty as an American to own one.

WHAT IS A SUPPRESSOR?

The simple answer to this question is "that thing on the muzzle that makes it quieter." Sure, and when you replace the current barrel on your rifle with one that is longer, it will be quieter. Not much, but it will be measurably quieter. Does that make a longer barrel a suppressor? Before you derisively answer, "Of course not, you moron," consider this: the government must have a definition, otherwise they are making it up as they go along. They get accused of that often enough as it is, and for the most part agents don't want to be the ones who make something up, only to be corrected, admonished and mocked in the office until they transfer.

So, the quick summary is this: a suppressor or silencer is an addition to a barrel that has a closed end, with room for the bullet to pass (or not, creating its own path, as with wipes) and causes a measurable decrease in sound levels.

A muzzle brake has a closed end, but it does not decrease sound, it increases it. A "bloop tube," a front sight extension tube, decreases sound (it is longer, it has to by the laws of physics) but it does not have a closed end. A longer barrel is just a longer barrel. There's a muzzle device known as a KX3 that is a large tube with an inverted cone inside of it. I looks like it might be a suppressor, and it does seem to take some of the blast out of the muzzle report from the shooter's perspective. But, it only re-directs muzzle blast and noise, and it is just as loud to the sides and even louder to the front. Thus, not a suppressor.

What about movie props, and the "hold my beer and look at this" approaches to silencers? Yep, silencers, and they are so even if they only last for one shot, like the plastic pop bottle trick you see now and then in movies.

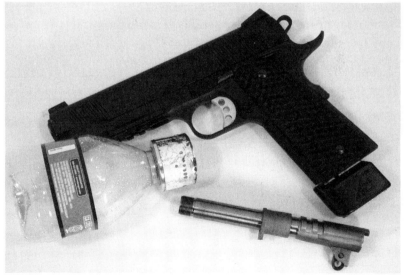

If you buy a suppressor, you need a host to mount it on. If you buy a pistol-caliber suppressor and do not have a threaded barrel on your handgun, you'll have to get one.

So if your buddy says he's found a loophole, an end-around to the government definition, don't believe him. He hasn't, and if he keeps posting those videos on his blog, some day he's going to find they are not so amusing.

WHAT DO WE CALL THEM?

The original term was "silencer." That's what Maxim called them, back when he invented them more than a century ago. For the longest time they were silencers and everyone was happy. But, they do not silence the gunshot, they simply decrease it. In some circles they were called "moderators," but that was, as far as I can tell, mostly a British usage. As Churchill commented, we're a people separated by a common language. Or was that George Bernard Shaw? Who can be certain? The point is, arguing over a name is silly and distracts us from the idea: suppressors are fun, and they protect our hearing.

A short while ago, in the scheme of things, a new term started cropping up; suppressors. They suppress the sound of a gunshot, they don't silence it, and that was the en vogue term for a while. Today, you can call them whatever you want, we've all had so much fun using them that no one really cares what you call them anymore. Silencer, suppressor, moderator if you want to be pretentious, it's all the same. I'll use suppressor for this book, mostly because that term that seems to be wired into my brain, but not because I'm wedded to one over the other. Don't get wrapped up in semantics, just have fun. And for god's sake don't correct someone else's usage. That's just rude.

CHAPTER 2

THE BIG FOUR:
COST, COMPOSITION, CALIBER & CONNECTION

• • •

COST

What does a suppressor cost and why? Several factors are involved: cost of materials of which it is composed and the service life expected of it (more on that in a bit); method of fabrication; size of the company involved and the volume of production; and relative demand and competition.

One term you'll run into is "full-auto-rated." This means you can heat the suppressor up to literal red-hot temps and it will still work. It will still be a suppressor when it cools down, and not a misshapen lump of metal that must be scrapped. This takes some pretty tough metals, and designs that won't sag or shift when heated to be that degree. Creating suppressors that perform at this level adds weight and cost, and is pretty hard on barrels.

The last time I tested such a device for television, I ran eight 30-round magazines through an M16, doing full auto, full magazine, 30-round "dumps" as quickly as I could re-load. The IR thermometer used to measure temperature at the end of the firing ran past 1,000 degrees Fahrenheit so quickly that the numbers were just a blur. The suppressor is still here and works fine. The barrel survived quite nicely, and the ammo was someone else's expense. (That's the beauty of TV, fun and the supplies are all on someone else's dime. Except for the working conditions, I recommend it.)

Still, not many of us need that level of durability.

It takes a lot of heavy machinery and experience to make a durable, long-serving, suppressor that works well. Anyone who makes it needs more than a couple of Chinese engine lathes in a garage. Real companies expect to make a living making things. So, you will find that real suppressors cost real money, in part because of the machines and experience needed to make them. As an example, in a world where a basic rifle suppressor costs $600 and a top-end, name-brand can runs twice that, someone who is selling suppressors at $250 for your AR might generate a bit of suspicion.

They could be good. They could be not-so-good. He might not be at the gun show the next time, who knows? If he's gone and the suppressor is awful, where can you go for help?

Last is supply and demand. When they were rare and fabulous and few states allowed them, suppressors that cost $1,200, $1,500, even $2,000 were not unheard of. Now that many more companies make them (every time I've gone to the SHOT show the last few years there have been more and more suppressor makers) simple economics will bring prices down. Also, when a really big player like Ruger gets involved, economy of scale can bring prices down as well.

As an example, if you are buying bar titanium to make suppressors and a big order is 100 feet of Grade 9, you are not going to get it at the same cost per foot as the bigger company that places a quarterly thousand-foot order. That's life. Worse yet, the small shop, with their annual 100-foot order, might even have to pay cash up front, while the company that buys in volume can buy on credit, which also brings the price down.

Generally speaking, if you spend more you will get a more capable suppressor. But that isn't a lock, as one I was just testing shows. The Sig SRD556QD at $695 it is a heck of a suppressor, illustrating what the muscle of a big company can do to prices.

COMPOSITION

You can't make suppressors out of just any old recycled material. Well, you can, and it happens in the movies, where someone picks up an discarded plastic soda bottle and uses it as an impromptu suppressor.

Been there, done that, got the registered parts to do it properly, and let me tell you, it is nothing like what Hollywood tells us. But that's a different chapter, book even.

Commercial suppressors are made of metal, and which metal they are made of depends on the desired application, caliber and service life.

Until synthetics experience a revolutionary improvement, we'll be making suppressors out of metal until we move up to lasers, particle beams, or phased plasma weapons.

As they say in awards ceremonies; the nominees are: aluminum, titanium, stainless steel, Inconel, Stellite and polymer.

ALUMINUM

A white, light metal, aluminum was almost unknown as a metal until the 19th century. The bottleneck was extracting it from its ore, most commonly bauxite, because it bonds so well with its oxidation partners. The strength of those bonds explains the conundrum: while aluminum is the most common metal in the planet, it was one of the last to be refined and used industrially. It took the development of electrical smelting to make it more than a rarity.

By itself, aluminum is too weak to be useful, so it is alloyed with other metals and elements. Chief among those are manganese, silicon, zinc, copper and magnesium.

The two common alloys are "aircraft aluminum" and "forged 7075" aluminum.

Aircraft aluminum is usually a 6061 alloy, with silicon, magnesium and copper. It is easily machined, durable, resistant to stress cracking, and corrosion-resistant. It is not, however, the strongest aluminum alloy, so while you will encounter it often in the handguards of your AR-15, it will not be what the receivers of your rifle are made of.

The other alloy is typically 7075, often the T6 version. 7075 is an alloy of zinc, magnesium, copper and chromium. The T6 means it has been treated to a particular process and sequence for hardness, and artificially aged to strengthen it.

7075 is stronger than 6061, more corrosion-resistant (although no aluminum alloy corrodes easily) but also more expensive due to the extra work treating it.

Aluminum is usually given a surface-hardening treatment known as anodizing. This is an electro-chemical surface prep where the surface of the parts are "passivated." Passivation involves treating the surface chemically to otherwise engage the molecular or crystalline sites where corrosion might begin, in effect "locking up" the potential corrosion spots. Think of it as locking the potential rust doors.

While strong and light, aluminum is not good at abrasion resistance and lacks a certain amount of torsion strength. A centerfire rifle cartridge, with high heat and high volume of expanding gases with particles in the mix, is a very abrasive experience for a suppressor. As a result, you will usually find aluminum used in suppressor baffles meant for use with rimfire firearms and pistol-caliber firearms. It can be used in the tube, but only with some sort of protection, such as skirted baffles, to keep the gases off the aluminum interior.

In the rimfire and handgun suppressors, the lower pressure and lower volume of gas permits the aluminum baffles to withstand the environment and not wear away. Also, it is difficult to heat a suppressor on a rimfire firearm to the point of strength reduction. It is possible on a pistol-caliber firearm, but it would have to be a sub machine gun, and you'd have to have a bushel basket of

Manufacturers buy raw materials in large quantities, and the larger the amount they buy, the better the price. But they have to buy the right stuff. Here's a rack of aluminum bars ready to be made into rimfire baffles.

loaded magazines ready to go.

As stated, it is possible to use aluminum as the external tube for a centerfire rifle suppressor designed to be as light as possible, at the expense of a full-auto rating. This would often be a hunting suppressor, and I would not be the least bit surprised to find someone in the near future making the external tubes out of a carbon fiber wrapping to lower weight even more. (As the ATF regulations require a stamped serial number, good luck getting the carbon fiber to accept stamping, and the ATF approving it.)

TITANIUM

Discovered at the end of the 18th century, titanium offers us a host of advantages. It is perhaps the most corrosion-resistant metal available to us, at least when you compare it to relatively low-alloy metals. It also offers one of the highest strength-to-weight ratios available.

Part of the corrosion-resistance of titanium is due to how quickly it oxidizes. No, that is not a contradiction. The surface of exposed Titanium will oxidize so quickly that it isn't possible to give it a surface treatment like bluing or anodizing. That, and the oxidized layer is impenetrable to further oxidation. Let's compare it to steel, as an example. Steel will rust, but the rust layer is not tightly bound to the substrate. As a result, it can rust underneath the rust, and will peel off in layers once sufficiently oxidized.

Titanium won't do that. However, there is a cost. If you try to weld titanium and do not properly protect the surface with an inert gas, the heat of welding will advance ahead of your bead, oxidize from the atmosphere, and that oxidation will harden the metal ahead of you. This leads to a bad weld, breaking parts, and a mess.

When properly welded, titanium welds so well that the welded area will not be visible afterwards. This is possible with aluminum, but not easy. This is almost impossible with steel.

Just to add to the difficulties of fabricating with titanium, it work-hardens at a stupendous rate. Work-hardening is where the part being bent or cut hardens and becomes brittle. Think of the last paperclip you just bent back and forth until you could break it. That's work-hardening in action. When you cut metal, the remaining metal, at the cut, has been work-hardened to one extent or another. Some alloys have such a low, controllable work-hardening rate that cutting it is simple. Titanium? Not a chance.

It takes a very particular machining rate – depth of cut, speed of cut across the surface, tool angle, lubricant type, flow and temperature, etc. – to cut titanium without work-hardening it ahead of the cut.

Titanium comes in alloys, known as grades, from 1 to 38. You will most likely encounter the lower-number grades, which is not to confuse them with lower-grade titanium.

The first four grades are unalloyed titanium and, as a soft metal, not much use for suppressors. But, they are also the most corrosion-resistant and they weld easily (with the appropriate equipment).

Grade 5 is alloyed with aluminum, vanadium and iron, and much stronger than chemically pure titanium. It is heat-treatable and used extensively in the aerospace industry, engine components, and the marine industry. It is very strong but difficult to work with.

Grade 9 is an alloy of aluminum and vanadium and offers a compromise between the weldability of 1-4 and the strength of 5.

There was for a short while great interest in using titanium to manufacture pistol frames, in particular 1911 frames. Titanium was described by my friend Ned Christiansen as "in-between aluminum and steel, but. In-between them in weight and in strength, but more expensive and a pain to work with."

I have a 1911 made with a titanium frame, and the big problem was galling. This is a sliding friction problem where the surfaces of the parts sliding across each other tear at each other, regardless of the lubricant used. I ended up having to treat the rails of the slide and frame with a surface coating of carbide to prevent galling.

Luckily for us there are no sliding parts in suppressors, so no worries about galling.

Titanium is used to reduce weight, maintain strength, and deal with heat. Due to the extreme difficulty in fabricating parts with it, it is used only in centerfire rifles, but not all of them, and those that use titanium will be expensive as a result.

STAINLESS STEEL

Okay, it isn't "stainless" and it isn't really "stain proof." Stainless can rust, but you really, really have to work at it, depending on the alloy.

First developed in the late 19th century, it wasn't until the early 20th century that manufacturing processes made it possible to produce stainless steel, steel that usually wouldn't rust, in quantity.

The basic problem is simple: you have to keep the carbon content down while larding in large amounts of nickel and chromium. There's also the little problem that metallurgists have to deal with: crystal size and shape. Stainless steel alloyed with nickel

Over on this rack, we have pre-hardened stainless steel, for baffles in something more than just rimfires.

and chromium but with the wrong iron crystals will rust. Rats.

The second problem is hardenability. If you just keep ladling in the nickel and chromium you can make a rust-proof metal. But it won't be a steel you can harden. If you take a quick look at the cutlery in your kitchen drawers, you might find some of it marked "18/8." This is an alloy with 18% chromium and 8% nickel, and while it is hard enough to work in forks and knives, it is soft enough that you can bend them with your bare hands. It cannot be heat-treated to be stronger.

But there are alloys that are very corrosion resistant that can be heat-treated, and these are used in suppressors.

The corrosion resistance of stainless is good, but the real reason we use it is strength. Nothing beats steel as long as weight isn't a problem. This strength comes at a secondary cost for us; stainless steel is a poor conductor of heat. (A bonus for cutlery, not so much suppressors.) Suppressors work by turning noise into heat and then soaking up the heat. A suppressor that won't soak up heat is one that is less effective, right? The lessened rate of heat conductivity is not so great that you can handle a stainless suppressor, but for those who want the best in a full-auto-rated can, stainless is a slight downgrade. At half the comparative thermal conductivity rate, you'll have a hard time measuring the decibel difference between a stainless steel suppressor and an identical one made of carbon steel.

Someone will eventually point out to you the difference, and you can immediately begin ignoring them for the rest of the conversation, perhaps forever. The potential loss of maybe a decibel, probably less than that, of sound reduction is well worth the corrosion resistance.

Stainless is designated with a three-digit numerical type, such as 304, 416 or 610. One of the 600 series is also known as 17-4, or 17-4PH. This is an alloy that can be treated by a process called precipitation hardening, and can be heat-treated for impressive strength. It offers great corrosion resistance along with ready machining, and as a result is favored by many in petroleum, chemical and aircraft industries.

A rifle-caliber suppressor made with 17-4PH will be very long-lasting, albeit a bit on the heavy side by a few ounces.

INCONEL

What if you took a mild steel and just kept adding nickel and chromium, and more nickel, and even more nickel? Along the way you tossed in some molybdenum or silicon, and even a bit of sulfur just to keep the mix from separating on you? You'd have made the superalloy known as Inconel. Inconel comes to us from the extreme-use crowd, that is, turbine engines, chemical processing plants, nuclear reactors and NASCAR.

Inconel is composed of nickel, anywhere from half to three-quarters of the Inconel composition is nickel, depending on the alloy. Then there are generous amounts of chromium, with dollops of iron, molybdenum and, in one particular alloy of Inconel, a bunch of cobalt.

Why do all this? Simple, corrosion-resistance to the max. The alloy works like other corrosion-resistant metals in that it forms a layer of oxidized metal on the surface, but in Inconel this layer is particularly thick and impervious.

If it is the wonder metal, why isn't it used in every suppressor? Well, there are a few reasons. One is cost. The wholesale price of Inconel depends on the size and shape and the amount you buy. A quick check turns up bars, 1.25 inches in diameter, which cost you $200 a foot. You can make enough baffles out of that for maybe two rifle suppressors. So, the bar, just sitting there, cost you $100 a suppressor before you even begin cutting on it. Then you have to machine it, and Inconel is as bad, or worse, than titanium when it comes to machining and work-hardening. You have to know what you are doing or you will scrap metal (at $100 per suppressor, ouch) and bust machine tools.

Even if you manage to buy and machine useable baffles, you still have to fit them inside of a tube and weld the whole thing together.

Inconel is great, but it is expensive, and you will notice that when you buy a suppressor that contains it. It is, however, one of the best materials you can use to make suppressor baffles, if you are willing to put up with the cost and weight. The main reason is that, barring a baffle strike, they are nearly indestructible. For those who need max performance, durability and heat-resistance-wise, Inconel is the go-to metal.

STELLITE

If Inconel still just isn't tough enough for you, then you have to go with Stellite. A trademarked name, Stellite is a cobalt-chromium alloy with large amounts of a few other metals, to include (but not all at the same time) iron, aluminum, carbon, boron, manganese, molybdenum, and traces of phosphorus, silicon and titanium.

The big advantage of Stellite is its resistance to wear and abrasion, even when being worked at extreme temperatures. It used to be common to press-fit a Stellite liner in machine gun barrels, just ahead of

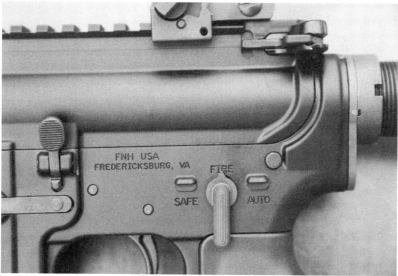

Some lucky few have select-fire rifles, and for them a full-auto-rated suppressor is a good idea. (Unless it is just cosmetic, then do you really need it?)

the chamber, to take the wear-and-tear of the heat and bullet friction when the barrel was red hot. This was just in front of the chamber, where the heat and wear were at their greatest. It is still called for in M240, 7.62 NATO machine gun barrels, in common use in the U.S. and many other military forces.

This abrasion resistance is just the best when installed in a suppressor. Of course, you have to ask yourself if the cost is worth it if you are never going to heat your suppressor up to red-hot temps. If you think for a moment, abrasion resistance makes the material difficult to machine as well. It is common, in the industrial applications where Stellite is used, to cast the alloy as a part as close to the usable dimensions as possible, and then grind it to final shape and fit.

The cost of the raw alloy isn't that great, only $40 a pound (at the latest quote) but the cost and hassle of shaping it makes it rare even in exotic suppressor circles. This is definitely something you do not need in a rimfire suppressor, for sure.

CALIBER

Suppressors are designed for a specific use. That is, they are made to fit a particular caliber because bullet size, gas flow and pressure matter. I don't care how good a 5.56 suppressor you own, if you put it onto a .308 rifle you are going to be very unhappy, very quickly. Try as it might, the bullet is not going to fit through the hole in the baffles and will end up making its own holes.

We're jumping ahead a bit here, but rimfire cans, 5.56 cans and 9mm ones will have the same thread pitch; one-half-inch in diameter, with threads pitched at 28 per inch. A rimfire suppressor screwed onto a 5.56 rifle will have a short and unhappy life, and it will be even shorter and messier if it is threaded onto a 9mm pistol. If at some point in the future you have any of these combinations in firearms and suppressors, be very, very careful what you put on where. And do not let your friends, relatives or gun club buddies at the range just screw on whatever suppressor fits. The results could be very bad, or at least, quite expensive.

A suppressor is designed for a particular volume and strength, according to the caliber it is meant to deal with. As a result, you'll see limitations from the manufacturer on a suppressor. "Rated for

Precision firearms need precision suppressors, and that's why there is such a price range in suppressors. Not just the materials, but the tolerances to which those parts are held.

.308 Remington, barrels longer than 12 inches" is one example. Or, "Rated for .300 RUM down to 16-inch barrel, .300 WinMag to 12 inches and .308 to 8-inch barrel lengths." They have designed and constructed a suppressor that can handle a certain amount of pressure and can deal with a certain maximum gas flow volume, and they are being up-front about what their suppressor will take.

Why? Simple, the noise you hear is caused by pressure. When the cartridge is fired, the chamber pressure is at its maximum, then the pressure goes down as the bullet moves forward, due to the increasing volume of the bore, with the bullet as the plug. When the bullet leaves, there is a certain pressure at the muzzle, called the "uncorking pressure," and that is what causes the noise we are trying to control.

The higher the initial pressure, the greater the residual pressure down the bore. The shorter the barrel, the higher the uncorking pressure, simply because the expansion volume of the bore hasn't increased enough to drop the pressure.

And here's the important part for those of you interested in putting a suppressor on your big boomers: the powder you use (or the ammo company uses) also makes a difference. A slow-burning or "progressive" powder acts to keep the bore pressure up as the bullet travels forward. That is part of how it gets you more velocity. (That, and a

If a suppressor maker makes more than one or two models, they need racks of bins of parts. Shades of Raiders of the Lost Ark.

higher starting pressure.) So, your .300 magnum, of whatever type, is going to not only burn more powder, but a slower-burning powder, than a .308 would, and this increases both the volume and uncorking pressure that a suppressor has to deal with.

That's why suppressors are rated for a minimum barrel length.

As long as you are within the pressure and volume limits the manufacturer lists, and at or under bullet diameter, you are okay. Your .308-rated suppressor will be just fine, and happy as a clam, if you put it onto your smaller-cartridge-case rifle or smaller-bullet-diameter rifle. That is, the 6.5 Creedmoor, 6.5 Grendel, .260 Remington, 243, etc. It will find a .223/5.56 rifle a piece of cake to deal with, being both smaller case and smaller bullet. However, it will not be as happy with a .270 Winchester or .280 Remington, and it will be very unhappy if you put it on a 7mm Remington magnum.

You have to consider bullet diameter, chamber pressure, case volume and expected burn rate of common powders if you are going to use a suppressor across cartridges and in different firearms.

When in doubt, drop a line to the manufacturer. They'll be happy to tell you if what you have in mind is okay or not. In fact, they'd prefer it if you ask ahead of time.

RIMFIRE CONSIDERATIONS

Rimfires are not just rimfires. There is the common and expected (but surprisingly sharp) .22LR. The Twenty-Two Long Rifle has a chamber pressure of 21,000 PSI, but the expansion ratio (the ratio of the case compared to the case plus bore when the bullet leaves the muzzle) is so great that pressure has dropped to perhaps the firearm's minimum by uncorking.

Change that to the .22 Magnum and things get more involved. Not because the expansion ratio is so much different, but that the magnum uses different powders and retains more pressure, garnering the extra velocity it is marketed for. Ditto the various .17s.

And then when you go to the 5.7x28, the FN cartridge, the case is a lot bigger, the expansion ratio is much smaller, and the uncorking pressure a lot more. As a result, some rimfire suppressors will be rated for the 5.7 and others will not.

As above, when in doubt, ask. Putting your perfectly fine and happy with your 10/22 rimfire suppressor on your buddy's SBR'd FN PS90 may make for a bulged or broken suppressor.

HANDGUNS

The common suppressor is for the 9mm, the most popular. There are others made for the .40 and .45, but they are less common. It is typical for someone who wants one suppressor to fit them all to buy a .45 and have rear cap adapters to fit it onto 9mm and .40 handguns. Yes, it has larger bore holes than would be called for in those applications, and thus will be a bit noisier, but it will amount to a decibel or few at most. That, compared to the cost savings of having just one, appeals to many.

RIFLES

Most people either get caliber-specific suppressors or they invest in one or two (or more). The common approach here is to buy a .308 and use it on everything .308 and smaller, including 5.56, and add a second one that will handle the big magnums, like the .300s, or even jump up to a .338 suppressor, which will laugh at the efforts of your biggest .300 magnum.

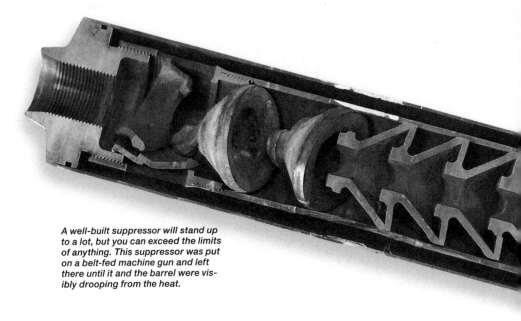

A well-built suppressor will stand up to a lot, but you can exceed the limits of anything. This suppressor was put on a belt-fed machine gun and left there until it and the barrel were visibly drooping from the heat.

MOUNTS

You can't just use duct tape and baling wire to secure a suppressor. There are two types: direct-thread and quick-detach (QD). Some manufacturers have begun making suppressors with a rear cap that is a socket, and you can then thread into the socket either a direct-thread or a QD system.

Why elaborate systems to keep the suppressor on? Simple, each time you shoot, the jet of gases flow out of the muzzle, behind the bullet, and crash into the first baffle, the first surface ahead of them in the expansion chamber. "Big deal," you say? Let's do a quick bit of math. If the uncorking pressure of your rifle is only 7,500 PSI, and the impact surface of the baffle in the expansion chamber is only one-half of a square inch in surface, then the suppressor gets hit with a jet of gas that generates 3,750 pounds of impact. Impact that is trying to drive the suppressor off the muzzle.

That's why you want good, sturdy threads on your barrel.

DIRECT THREAD

This is exactly what is sounds like. An example would be a 5.56 rifle with the muzzle threaded for 1/2-28. The rear cap of the suppressor would be threaded 1/2-28, and you simply screw the suppressor on (after taking off the flash hider, if any) and tightening it to stay.

The advantages of direct-thread are obvious: it is less expensive, it is lighter and it is durable. The disadvantages are equally obvious: you have to spin your suppressor for as many turns as it takes to get it tight. If the thread pitch is 28 tpi, and you have half an inch of threaded shank, then it will be fourteen turns to tight.

Tight for a rifle suppressor is not just hand-tight. You will want to use a wrench to generate enough inch-pounds of torque to keep the suppressor on tight.

If you have one rifle and you won't be using your suppressor on any other, then direct-thread is a no-brainer. If you are going to use it on more than one, then it is a decision between you and your wallet as to your choice. The options are: buy a suppressor for each rifle; keep a wrench handy to swap suppressor or suppressors around on your rifles; or buy a suppressor that uses a QD mount and install those mounts on each rifle so you can quickly swap the suppressor.

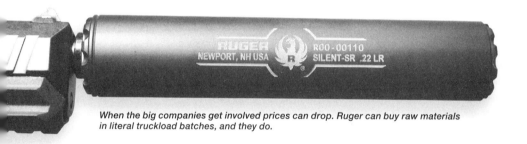

When the big companies get involved prices can drop. Ruger can buy raw materials in literal truckload batches, and they do.

QUICK-DETACH

This also, obviously, means quick-attach. The process is simple. The manufacturer makes a device that threads onto your barrel. This device has a set of threads or a quick-lock system that the suppressor latches onto. You can screw the suppressor onto the mount with a turn and a half. Or, slide it on and turn the locking collar a half-turn to lock on the suppressor.

The advantages are several. First, you can have a flash hider or muzzle brake on your rifle, even when the suppressor is off, if that's how the mount is made (and many are).

You can swap your suppressor from one rifle (or handgun) to another quickly, without the use of tools. Of course, this supposes the

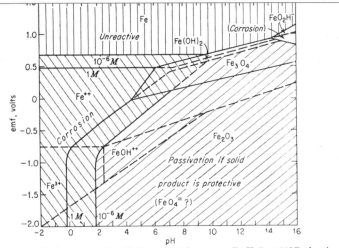

FIG. 10-5. Equilibrium potential–pH diagram of the system Fe-H₂O at 25°C, showing areas of corrosion, passivation, and no reaction under a partial pressure of one atmosphere of oxygen. The solid lines bound the equilibria for the stable products, Fe, Fe_3O_4, Fe_2O_2, FeO_2H. The ranges in which intermediate products predominate are bounded by dashed lines. For the procedure in calculating this diagram see the Pourbaix reference.

Knowing what it takes to create a suppressor, and how to protect it from corrosion, can involve more than a few weekends of experimenting. It takes a lot of classroom time just to parse out what a diagram like this means, let alone use it to improve the suppressors you are making. Quality costs for a reason.

suppressor is cool, as you won't be swapping a suppressor bare-handed when it is at 700 degrees.

The big deal with this is economics. I just did the arithmetic with a suppressor that happens to be on my desk as I write this, a Sig SRD556QD. Sig makes the same suppressor as a direct thread, the SRD556.

The SRD556QD lists at $695 and mounts are $60 each. The SRD556 is $545. By the time you buy two SRD556 suppressors, you could have bought one SRD5566QD and six extra mounts. If you have that many .223/5.56 rifles, you can swap one suppressor between them.

The downsides are also simple: a QD-built suppressor is going to cost more than a plain direct-thread model. (That is, manufacturer-specific, model-alike.) Also, because of the mount and the rear of the suppressor that has to be machined for it, the QD model will be a bit heavier than the direct-thread version. In the case of the ones just used as a comparison, the SRD556 weighs 11.5 ounces and the SRD556QD weighs 14 ounces.

CHAPTER 3

COST & MATERIAL CONSIDERATIONS

· · · ·

How much does a suppressor cost? It's as much or as little as you wish to spend. You can probably find a .22 rimfire suppressor for as little as $300, and a top-end one for a centerfire rifle will be over $1,500. A big magnum-rated suppressor, such as something for a .338 Lapua, can easily top $2,000 and one for a .50 BMG will set you back $2,500. Those are not pricey because the makers figure if you can afford a .338 or a .50, you can afford an expensive suppressor. In reality, it takes a lot to handle the gas volume of those big cartridges, and engineering, design and materials cost money.

Not a useful price range, right?

As with many things, you get what you pay for, and you pay for what you get. The more expensive a suppressor, the more likely you are of getting one from a company what will back it if anything goes wrong. A company that has done their due diligence in design, materials selection, fabrication and testing. Spending more for a better suppressor is rarely a bad choice, just a more-expensive one.

But this isn't just about the cost of the suppressor. You will have a choice, you will have a budget, you will have needs and desires, and you will be able to settle on a suppressor.

What we'll consider here are the ancillary costs, the costs no one mentions when you are thinking of buying a suppressor.

What might those be? How about this for starters, will the firearm you want to put a suppressor on actually accept one? If, for example, you want to have a 9mm suppressor for your handgun because it is cool and it will be fun and the guys at the gun club will be envious, ask yourself this: is the barrel threaded on the handgun you now own? If it isn't, you have to solve that problem sooner or later, but certainly before you step onto the firing line at the gun club.

You can solve that problem by buying a replacement barrel, but now you've just added that cost to the price of a suppressor. Some pistols (you won't find many revolvers with suppressors on them, regardless of what the movies show) make that easy. A drop-in barrel, longer and threaded, is easy to source. Glock, Sig, S&W, the list is extensive. Those who own a 1911 might not find it so easy, but you can find them.

Is your pistol suited to a suppressor? If your one-and-only handgun is a Glock 43, the ultra-compact 9mm, you are going to find a distinct shortage of threaded, suppressor-ready barrels for it.

If you do not have a handgun that can accept a suppressor-ready barrel, then you'll have to buy one. Which should mean, if you are being rational about it, something that comes right from the factory with a threaded barrel. (Don't go about solving the problem twice, right?) So now, instead of a $150-200 replacement barrel you've jumped up to a $600 purchase just to have a firearm on which you can put a suppressor.

I don't mean to be insulting, but I've run into people who haven't thought this through and find themselves, having already ordered a suppressor, starting another search, looking for a suitable "host" onto

Once you have your suppressor (or even before) you need a firearm that will accept it. Thankfully, a lot of firearms manufacturers are aware of this and are starting to offer suppressor-ready firearms as catalog items.

which the soon-to-arrive suppressor will be mounted.

Firearms manufacturers are now a lot more able to handle your needs. A lot of models, when they are released, are offered in full size, compact, and threaded-for-suppressor variants.

Before we settle this "easy" problem, there is the matter of sights. Typically, a pistol suppressor will be large enough in diameter that, when mounted, it blocks the regular sights on your pistol. Suppressor-ready pistols not only come with an extended, threaded, barrel, but taller sights. If your pistol does not have them, you'll have to install them or have a gunsmith install them. More cost, added to the suppressor. Don't blame me, I'm just pointing these things out.

For rifles the problems are a mixed bag. Unless you live in a state where threaded muzzles are not allowed, every AR made that you can buy will already be threaded for something on the muzzle. But what about the bolt-action rifle you use for varmint shooting? Or your deer-hunting rifle?

If your rifle does not have threads on the muzzle it is not an easy thing to correct. Misaligned threads are worse than no threads, as you'll damage a suppressor if the alignment is off enough (and it doesn't take much misalignment to be "enough"). Not just anyone can cut threads that will properly align. In the old days I'd have said

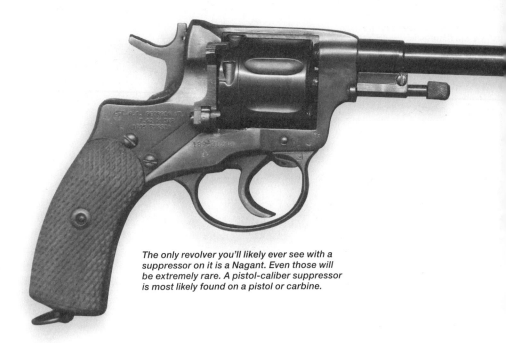

The only revolver you'll likely ever see with a suppressor on it is a Nagant. Even those will be extremely rare. A pistol-caliber suppressor is most likely found on a pistol or carbine.

you would be better off finding a real machinist to cut the threads, rather than a lot of the gunsmiths out there. But, gunsmiths have upped their game since a lot more customers are looking for threaded muzzles.

But it will still cost you. You need precision, and it takes a really big lathe to accept a barreled action for threading. If the lathe isn't big enough, the gunsmith/machinist has to remove the barrel from the action in order to chuck it up in the lathe and thread it. And big or small, the lathe has to be precise enough (and the machinist careful enough) to make the threads centered and straight.

This can cost you $100 to 200, depending on the person cutting and how involved the work has to be to get it done right. And there's the risk, albeit small, of some cosmetic damage to your rifle from the chuck jaws, and from removing and re-installing the barrel.

This is why a lot of new suppressor owners buy a new rifle as the host for their soon-to-arrive suppressor. It is just easier than getting an existing unthreaded barrel ready to go by having it threaded.

As we'll cover in Chapter Ten, you'll have to clean your suppressor. This can be as simple as taking it apart and scrub thoroughly before re-assembly (which gets old fast) or an ultrasonic cleaning machine.

That's another $100 to $500, and a place to store it, or a countertop or workbench to leave it on.

If you have a direct-thread suppressor, you'll need the correct size wrench or wrenches to install, remove and swap it.

We'll cover this in detail in Chapter Nine, but if you plan to install a suppressor, you must (and I really am insistent on this point) invest in a Geissele alignment rod. It is $65, and it can save you the cost, time and heartache of a busted suppressor.

If you have a QD-design suppressor, make sure you can stand the cost of mounts, so you can swap your suppressor from one rifle to another. This can be $60, it can be $180, and they are model-dependant. That is, company A makes a QD mount suppressor and mount, and Company B also makes one, but they do not work with each other's suppressors. Stop complaining, you can't expect the replacement parts for Fords, Chevys and BMWs to interchange, can you? So why would you expect, in an industry as new and small as the suppressor industry, to find a universal QD mount design to adopt?

You will need wrenches to mount the mount or the direct-thread suppressor, and while they aren't absolutely necessary, the dies and taps of the thread patterns you will be using can be handy. If you go to remove a mount and the threads are all gunked up from the previous mount's thread-locking compound, you want that stuff off before you mount the next one. They can make life easier, when you are swapping suppressors

Some barrels cannot easily be threaded. The rifle barrel on the left not only needs to be threaded to accept a suppressor, but needs the front sight moved or removed.

If you will be mounting suppressors on ARs, it is a whole lot easier if you have a reaction rod.

from one firearm to the next.

Buy lost-cost but not lousy wrenches, and do not be afraid to slap them against a bench grinder if you need to make one thinner to reach the flats of a mount or flash hider.

Given the time and effort it took to acquire your new gizmo, you might want to consider a safe (if you don't already have a gun safe). Even something relatively compact can be bolted to the rafters of your basement and be big enough to hold your suppressor. It would be bad enough to have to report to the local police that there was a burglary and your guns were taken, but imagine the hassle of reporting a stolen suppressor? And if the local newspaper or TV station gets wind of it? No, you don't need that hassle.

Wrenches are a must. Get the right size, get more than one, and modify them if you must.

You now have more than just a hunting rifle to store, so you might want to start thinking of a safe, like these from Stack-On. Hint: get one bigger than you think you need, because you will get more firearms and suppressors, and once you have a safe, you discover things that should be locked up that you hadn't thought of before.

You can buy a small one, a lockbox, for a couple of hundred dollars. Or, this can be the impetus you needed to get a real-deal gun safe, one big enough to hold all your firearms. Especially since, with a new suppressor, you'll be adding firearms just so you can put the suppressor on them. Trust me, I've seen it happen.

You may want to add a suppressor cover to the gear. A suppressor cover is a non-flammable wrap that goes around the suppressor. It does a couple of things. First, it greatly reduces the chance that you will burn yourself on a hot suppressor. Since the front cap will be blazing hot (hotter than it would be without the wrap, it is an insulator after all) you can still burn yourself. Second, it cuts down on mirage from the heat of the suppressor, the heat that would be wafting up in your line of sight. It doesn't eliminate it, since, again, the front cap is hot, but it does cut it down. And in certain social circles it is almost a requirement.

You will find yourself being more particular about your ammunition once you own a suppressor. Putting some heavy-weight 5.56 bullets down the barrel of your slow-twist older AR is an "oops" moment at the range, once you realize why you aren't hitting the target. Doing that with a suppressor on the end will almost certainly lead to a

A suppressor cover blocks most of the heat, but not all. And, it blocks none of the burning oil that comes out of your cleaned suppressor, the first time you shoot it after a scrubbing.

baffle strike before you notice the "no holes in the target" symptoms. As a result, you'll be less likely to use low-cost reloaded ammo or borrowed ammo from your buddy. The fun quotient will go way up, but the cost per shot will take a tick up as well.

I don't mean to scare you or drive you off of the potential purchase of a suppressor, but I wouldn't be honest if I didn't point out that buying the suppressor might only be half or less of the cost of embarking on a new chapter in shooting.

What should your suppressor be made of? After all, that is part of the cost, and what it is made of matters in cost as well as function. What it should be made of depends on how you plan to use it. Let's take two extremes, one, a hunter, and another, a seriously focused, class-attending, skill-building shooter.

The hunter will in all likelihood select as light a suppressor as will stand up to the caliber he or she is using. That means an aluminum tube with titanium baffles, maybe even a sealed unit, and direct thread. The hunter thus will need the alignment rod, an open-end wrench and a suppressor wrap for camouflage. That's it, unless there's a need for a safe. Hunters can get off easy, here.

The high-volume class shooter will probably want either a suppres-

Extra pistol barrels don't help if they aren't extended and threaded. Extended and threaded barrels don't help if they have a permanently attached muzzle brake or comp on them. But a spare, fitted, barrel, is what you need, and will have to get.

sor entirely made of titanium or one that is full-auto rated (even if he doesn't have a full-auto firearm) with Inconel or Stellite inside. It will be heavy, it will be durable and it will be expensive. But, it will stand up to everything he or she can put through it in a class. This shooter will need a QD suppressor with mounts for the other rifles. He'll need the alignment rod, a cleaning tank if he cleans, wraps, the whole shebang.

As a general guide, the following rules will get you started, and maybe even see you through to a new suppressor or several.

RIMFIRES

Aluminum rules for rimfires, as there is no reason to use anything stronger for the external tube. The baffle stack can be aluminum (monocore designs particularly) or stainless steel. No need for exotics, unless you want to have something that can stand up to .22 magnums, .17s and the 5.7. Even then, an aluminum tube and stainless baffles will get the job done.

HANDGUN

Here again, aluminum rules. The various centerfire handgun cartridges (in rimfire handguns you use a rimfire suppressor, obviously) do not have sufficient uncorking pressure to be a problem. You'll find that all handgun suppressors use an aluminum tube (except for those who want to show off with a titanium tube) and the common baffle material is stainless steel. You can save some weight with a set of titanium baffles, but since you'll be using a booster to ensure the handgun cycles, the weight difference between stainless baffles and titanium ones matter only to your hands and holster.

Often, for reasons of durability, the end caps of an aluminum handgun suppressor will be made of stainless steel. The regular thread-on, thread-off work of installing it clearly calls for steel. And the front cap, usually the place you start disassembly, works better with the included wrench for unscrewing, especially if you have neglected it and have to force it loose.

SMALL & MEDIUM CENTERFIRE RIFLE

This is where all the anguish, drama and decision making comes in. You see, a whole lot of people think that aluminum just isn't the deal you want for a hard-use 5.56 suppressor. Yes, you can find them, and you may well be happy with one. But in their opinion you will have to be careful with it. And, it will not be as light as you might like. You see, aluminum isn't as strong as steel, and in order to maintain a safety margin, a suppressor maker who uses aluminum in an external tube will have to use thicker walls.

That might have been the case a few years ago, but the manufacturers have solved that problem, and now aluminum-tube 5.56 suppressors are common.

But a lot of 5.56 (and that is by far the biggest segment of the market) suppressors will be stainless steel or exotic alloys, as in an all-stainless suppressor, or a stainless tube with Inconel or Stellite baffles, or titanium tube and stainless baffles, or titanium inside and out.

A typical mix (if anything in the suppressor industry could be considered "typical") would be a stainless steel mount and front cap, an aluminum tube, and Stellite or Inconel baffles. But, if you want a hard-use suppressor and you want it without breaking the bank, then an all-stainless one will serve you for many, many years.

THE BIG .30S

When you get to the big bores (and for our purposes, we'll consider a .308-inch bullet, one that goes into a big-bore rifle), two things matter: is it a magnum and how short is the barrel. Magnums and .30 SBRs will require much tougher builds than non-magnums and hunting-length barrels. Your .300 Winchester magnum with a 20-inch barrel is hard on a suppressor, but probably not any harder than a .308 with an 11-inch barrel.

THE REAL BIG BOOMERS

The big ones are those meant for cartridges including the .338 Lapua Magnum and up. These are specialized, and you aren't going to have a lot of choices when it comes time to put a suppressor on, say, your .50 BMG rifle. And, should you find the perfect suppressor for your .458 Socom, do not for a moment assume it will be happy if you somehow park it on a .458 Winchester magnum.

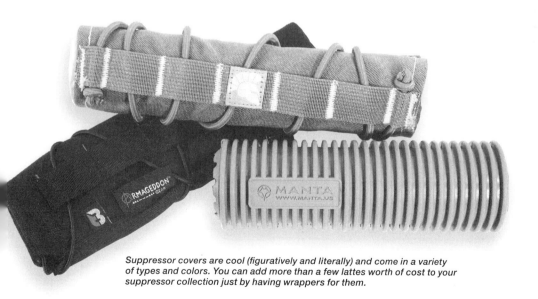

Suppressor covers are cool (figuratively and literally) and come in a variety of types and colors. You can add more than a few lattes worth of cost to your suppressor collection just by having wrappers for them.

Specialized cartridges call for specialized suppressor designs and builds, and there won't be much, if any, overlap. You might find that you can get along fine using a compact .30 suppressor on your AR-15 in 5.56, but a .50 BMG suppressor (as one example) is a real brute. It can weigh nearly five pounds, be a foot and a half long, and cost you $2,500. You aren't going to put that on any lesser rifle and use it.

Generally speaking, the more you use it and the more you move it around, the more you will need in the way of cleaning and support equipment. Your first suppressor may only cost you $600, but the extra gear can cost that much as well. The second suppressor? That won't take any extra support gear, unless you've changed calibers, and then you'll need a new alignment rod.

Different sizes for different calibers means different wrappers/covers, and different mounts. An un-mounted suppressor doesn't do you much good.

CHAPTER 4

HOW QUIET IS QUIET?

• • •

First, how loud is loud? Noise – sounds, music, your annoying neighbor's radio – is the result of compression waves in the air. These travel from the source to and past you at the speed of sound. (Well, duh on the speed, but still necessary for purposes of definition.)

The compression of this wave is the sound level of the noise, measured in decibels (dB). The decibel scale is logarithmic, which means that when you increase a sound by ten decibels you have increased it by a factor of ten. That is, 70 dB is 10 times the power of 60 dB, and 80 dB is 100 times the power of 60 dB.

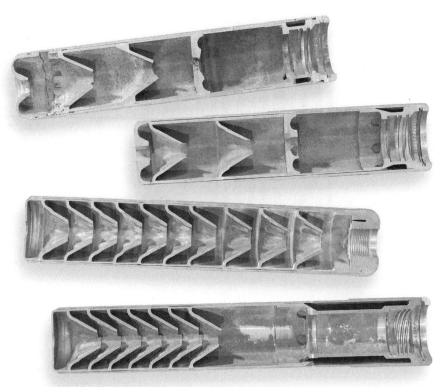

Some suppressors are quieter than others. This is due to design, materials, barrel length, powder used and the range you are on.

Noise causes hearing loss depending on exposure. There is no simpler explanation and no way to escape it. There is no "getting used to it" or "letting your ears get harder" or anything else. Stress does not reduce the physical toll noise takes, despite what hunters might tell you.

In this regard, noise is similar to what is explained in chemistry class: dose makes the poison. With some poisons you can shrug off a small dose. With others you can build up a tolerance. With others there is no "safe" dose, any exposure will kill you.

Noise is kind of like that. The gentle breeze, blowing through the leaves on the tree above your hammock, will not make you deaf no matter how much you listen to it. But, get a shock of 180 decibels and you will have lost some hearing, permanently.

Decibels? The unit of noise was named after Alexander Graham Bell, and the bel is a basic unit of sound measure. A decibel is one-tenth of a bel.

How noisy is noise? The government department in charge of these

Just the breeze through the trees can register over sixty decibels.

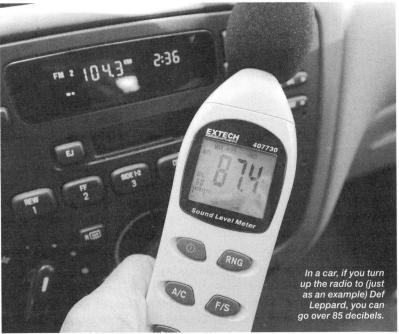

In a car, if you turn up the radio to (just as an example) Def Leppard, you can go over 85 decibels.

things, OSHA, deems 90 dB to be the maximum exposure in an eight-hour working day. 140 dB is deemed the level at which momentary exposure begins to cause hearing damage. As with many things, duration matters, in this instance a great deal, as we'll see.

The noise level of a lot of loud things has been measured, at various times and places, and we can construct a rough scale:

Average rifle shot .... 165 dB
Jet engine .... 150 dB
Rock concert, front row .... 130 dB
Jackhammer .... 120 dB
Snowmobile .... 120 dB
Rock concert, mid-arena .... 115 dB
Chainsaw .... 110 dB
Motorcycle (not a Harley) .... 100 dB
Inside your car, radio cranked up .... 85 dB
Vacuum cleaner .... 80 dB
Movies silencer sound .... 70 dB
Normal speech .... 60 dB

Keep in mind that time of exposure also matters. Yes, a chainsaw is "only" 110 dB, but unlike a gunshot, which is a microsecond exposure, you will be cutting wood for minutes to an hour. All power tools are in the 110 to 120 dB range, so your lawn mower, gas leaf blower (the electrics are a bit quieter), standing generator, etc. are all bad for your hearing, due to exposure time. As much as motorcycle riders talk about "noise is safety," it is also bad for their hearing. (Granted, it is less-bad than getting hit by a car or truck, but there must be a way to have both safety situations.)

To get a sense of relative loudness, when two people try to talk, standing three feet apart, over background noise:
with background noise at 40 dB, they can hear each other whispering
at 70 dB, they can hold a conversation at normal voice levels
at 90 dB, they have to raise their voices, but not shout
at 100 dB, they have to shout to be heard
at 105-110 dB, they cannot hold a conversation, and must get closer
Keep in mind this is with a constant background noise. Also note the last point: to be heard, they have to get closer. Distance matters. Given

Ear plugs are good and work in a lot of situations. Sometimes you need more.

enough distance, sound dissipates and eventually disappears into the background noise. At the firing line, everyone must wear hearing protection. But, 100 yards away at the gun club entrance the noise is lessened enough that they do not. My home gun club is an example. A nearby club, 1.25 miles away, regularly has the State Police practicing. You can easily identify them at practice and tell when they are shooting handguns, rifles, shotguns and, particularly, machine guns. But the noise, while recognizable, does not stir the needle of a sound meter over the background noise of the breeze in the trees.

Time of exposure and distance are protections, as well as plugs and muffs or a suppressor. OSHA has exposure times as well. Below the threshold of 80 Db, you can work an 8-hour day and they don't care. Above 90 dB, they insist you have hearing protection. For each dB increment above 90 dB they insist on a decreasing time of exposure, until at 115 dB you are only allowed an exposure to the noise for fifteen minutes.

Manufacturers have to work hard to make employees wear hearing protection and make sure they do not suffer overtime exposure, or there will be consequences.

Gunshots are momentary exposures, but once they are over 140 dB that moment is long enough to have an effect. So, we go to suppressors to tame the noise.

You'll read many numbers on suppressor makers' websites, and it may be a bit confusing. Many talk of "hearing safe" noise levels. This is a general term used to describe the muzzle blast decibel measurement minus the amount the suppressor reduces noise. If the total is under 140 it is considered "hearing safe."

Remember, exposure matters. If you have a momentary noise level at 130 dB, that is not like standing in the front row of a rock concert. One is a millisecond, the other is two hours.

All things being equal, a bigger suppressor is quieter than a smaller one. But, not all things are equal, and size is only a partial clue.

However, not all noise comes from the muzzle. A bullet traveling at supersonic velocities creates its own noise, the "sonic boom," or in the case of firearms, the "sonic crack." This is created by the bullet passing through the air, pushing the air aside and creating a compression wave. When the bullet is traveling faster than the speed of sound, the compression wave it creates takes on a new nature and becomes distinctly noticeable.

You can hear it when you have (and sooner or later you will) a cartridge that produces just enough velocity that the bullet is sometimes supersonic, and sometimes not. Some shots will "crack" and some will just be a dull thud. The classic case of this is a rimfire rifle with .22LR ammo that is right at the speed of sound. The normal distribution of velocities, shot to shot, will have some supersonic and some subsonic. Just to make things a bit more confusing, the speed of sound varies slightly with temperature and air density.

It is generally considered that the energy produced and delivered to your ears by the sonic crack is not enough to cause hearing harm. However, if you were to shoot tens of thousands of rounds of supersonic but suppressed rounds, unprotected, there might be some hearing loss.

To be truly quiet, a suppressed firearm has to be fed subsonic ammunition. Ammo makers are more and more aware of this, and the offerings will only increase.

A smaller suppressor will be louder, but then, for pistols, a smaller one doesn't need a booster. And this one on the left, a Thompson Machine Poseidon, can be run wet.

We don't know, no one has tested it yet, as far as I know.

Getting the sound below the 140 dB threshold is attainable even with the loudest firearms. However, there are limits. Let's take as an example a common setup: you have a really good suppressor on a full-sized AR-15 rifle. The 20-inch barrel bare produces a 160 dB muzzle blast. Your really good suppressor reduces noise by 35 dB. That creates a 125 dB signature (the fancy term for the noise you make) and it is hearing safe. In fact, it is pretty darned quiet.

A quick data point: the muzzle blast level and the suppressed levels are both measured one meter to the left of the muzzle, at a ninety-degree angle. Both are five feet above a level grassy surface. The measurement device is a meter away from the muzzle, and your ear is just about that far away, also.

Now, let's take another common setup, one that will be much less pleasant. You are shooting an AR-15 SBR, a short-barreled rifle, one with a common 11.5-inch barrel. The bare muzzle blast is 170 dB. The suppressor takes 35 dB off that and you are still safe at 135 dB. Why did the noise go up?

The shorter barrel releases the bullet sooner, when the bore pressure is higher than it is at the end of the 20-inch barrel. The higher pressure means a higher dB measurement. But here's the kicker, the measurements are still taken one meter from the muzzle, but your ear is now closer to the muzzle than it was before. Where your ear was 35-36 inches away before, now it is only 25 inches or so from the muzzle. Those lost 10 inches might add a couple of decibels to the noise your ear experiences, and you are now really close to the threshold of hearing-safe.

There are limits to just how quiet we can make a firearm.

Dr. Phil Dater measures the setup to make sure the microphone is one meter to the left of the muzzle.

Gunshots are measured one at a time with everything recorded, because it all matters. Not doing it right is worse than not doing it.

A single-shot, or a bolt-action rifle, has no extra noise besides the gunshot. A self-loading rifle adds its own action noises to the mix. The "clack" of an AR-15 action closing is 120 dB all by itself. "Whoa, waitaminit, it is as noisy as a snowmobile?" Yes, for the millisecond it lasts. If you were to put the world's most effective suppressor on an AR and feed it the quietest ammunition made, you still cannot get the noise of it down below 120 dB. But, it won't be recognizable as a gunshot.

Shorter barrels are louder, in part because the uncorking pressure is higher. This also puts more stress on a suppressor, so make sure yours is rated for a barrel as short as the one you want to put it on.

A secondary source of noise, one you will be vastly amused by when you first hear it, is the noise of the bullet striking the backstop. The "thump" of the bullet hitting dirt is loud, once you take the muzzle blast out of the signature. And falling steel plates? You'll probably want to put your hearing protection back on after a few shots on those. The clang of the steel is loud enough to be annoying, even when having fun shooting a suppressed firearm.

HOW TO MEASURE

It takes expensive equipment to accurately measure gun shots. Oh, someone will show up with an app on their smartphone and tell you how good it is. I ran into this when I first started shooting with suppressors. A police officer (this was in an LE Patrol Rifle class) showed me his app. We were standing on the range with rifles being fired, so we tested it. Standing at the shoulder of a student on the firing line, the smartphone app told us the gunshots we were hearing came out at a reading of 105 dB and there was not a suppressor on his rifle. We did not take our hearing protection off.

No app can measure a gunshot, and the low-cost noise meters you can buy won't either. They'll work

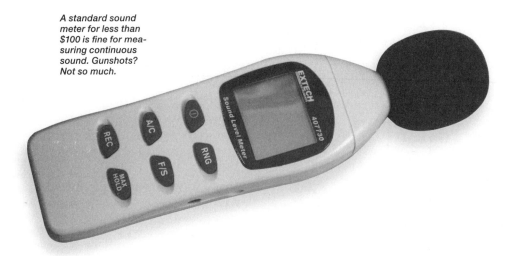

A standard sound meter for less than $100 is fine for measuring continuous sound. Gunshots? Not so much.

just fine on background noise and continuous noises. The reason for this is response time. It takes time for a microphone to respond to a noise and produce a signal that the circuitry can use. A microphone that can respond quickly enough to measure gun shots is an expensive one, and a noise meter that can handle the bandwidth needed to handle the information flow is also expensive.

To give you an idea, an app to measure noise costs you nothing, but you have to use a $1,000 smartphone. You're limited to the microphone in the phone. A standard meter will cost you $80 to $200, and it also will not have a fast-enough response time. A professional meter that can accurately measure sound levels of gun shots will easily run you $3,500 and requires annual calibration and certification.

One such piece of gear is a Larson-Davis model LXT1-QPR which, with the required microphone, calibration gauge, software and manuals, runs over $3,500. If you don't know the process to use it properly, you won't get accurate readings, regardless of how expensive the equipment is, so there's a learning curve to deal with as well.

So when your gun club buddy crows about his "super-quiet suppressor" and tells you he used his smartphone and app to determine it is "Only 110 dB, really quiet," you can nod and know he's wrong. Don't be a smart-alec and show him up in front of the crowd, not if you value your friendship. Just have him read this book. And keep your hearing protection on until you've had a chance to find out for yourself if his new suppressor really is a quiet one.

This is the base unit, a Larson-Davis sound meter capable of measuring gun shots.

The Larson-Davis meter, with microphone, calibrator and software. Then there's the storage case, the manuals, the regular calibration trip to the lab. Measuring gunshots is not something you can do with an app on your phone.

WET VS. DRY

You'll see that some suppressors are listed as "wet" suppressors. Your basic suppressor is an empty, dry tube. Well, empty except for the baffles, but not containing any substance not built-in. Suppressors work by allowing the gases to expand and cool. With a bit of water or an aqueous gel in there, there is more mass to cool, but also there is the matter of phase transition. It takes one calorie to change one gram of water to become one degree centigrade warmer. However, it takes 540 calories to change one gram of water already at 100 degrees

Celsius into one gram of steam. That's a lot of cooling. Basic math will tell you that if you start with air-temperature water, let's call it 72 degrees Fahrenheit, or 22 Celsius, it takes 80 calories per gram to bring that water to boiling. And another 540 to turn it into steam.

As a result, a "wet" suppressor (one that is both designed for and containing water or gel) will be quieter. This can be water or a gel known as "wire-drawing gel" that won't run out. And, you can only use a bit, because if you fill the suppressor, well, water is an in-compressible substance. Too much water makes for too much pressure inside the suppressor and things break.

However, as the author Robert Heinlein pointed out, there's no such thing as a free lunch.

If you put water or gel into a suppressor, you have to keep it there. If it drains out, it is useless. It gets used up as you shoot, so your suppressor gets slightly louder on each shot. And, they are messy. The water combines with the powder residues to create a black, oily substance that splatters on each shot. If you want to look like you just worked a shift in a coal mine, then shoot a wet suppressor for an afternoon.

There is another, very specialized application for a wet suppressor. If you happen to work in a wet environment, like you have just come up out of the water and you have a suppressed firearm, then you may want to use a suppressor constructed so that

A wet suppressor needs a heat-soaking liquid foam or gel inside to disperse the extra heat.

having water in it won't hurt it. Hmmm, I think we can imagine a job that has that requirement, can't we?

You can't just put water into any suppressor. The makers have designed for or tested with wet applications, and they will tell you if the model you own or are looking at is approved for wet use. If it isn't, don't.

If someone is exclaiming about how quiet their wet suppressor is, you may want to move away or at least get upwind, because there will be splatter. And if their suppressor wasn't made to be used wet, there may be breakage.

HOW QUIET IS QUIET ENOUGH?

Should you obsess over the dB ratings of suppressors? No, not really. The measured level of a suppressor can vary a few dB from day to day, depending on the temperature, air pressure and humidity. That's even before you start changing ammunition, as powders and the amount used to generate a given velocity can also have a large effect on the noise you hear. If you really wanted to know if one was better than another, you'd need the professional equipment, used by someone who knows how to use it, testing the different suppressors on the same firearm, with the same ammo, on the same day, and before the atmospheric conditions changed too much.

For our purposes, close enough is close enough. If someone says their suppressor delivers a 36 dB reduction and someone else says theirs delivers a 35 dB reduction, they are the same. It takes about a 3 dB difference before a practiced ear can start telling the difference between two suppressors. And that's before we even consider the change in the nature of the noise. If you change the pitch of a noise, you can reduce or increase its apparent sound level, as our ears are not equally sensitive across all frequencies. But that gets us perilously close to a graduate-level discussion of noise, and we're just looking to buy a good suppressor.

The important info you need to take away from this chapter is this: anyone who is in the business of making suppressors today makes good ones. They have to, the competition is too fierce to make bad ones any more.

FIRST ROUND POP

What is this mysterious thing called first round pop? When you fire your handgun or rifle (there are shotgun suppressors, but they are rarities even in the suppressor world), you blast a stream of hot gases out of the muzzle and into the suppressor. The hot gases also contain particulates, small bits of ash or powder residue. These gases and particulates become incandescent in the atmosphere. That is the main cause of the muzzle flash you see, not "unburned powder." It is incandescent, just like the filament in the light bulbs you are replacing with LEDs and fluorescents. And that filament does not burn up, does it?

On the first shot, the air inside of the suppressor is just like that of the outside; it contains oxygen, usually at the 20–21% level. (If not, you have bigger problems than how loud your suppressor will be.)

When these hot gases hit the air in the suppressor, the oxygen in the air supports the incandescence of the gases and particulates. They

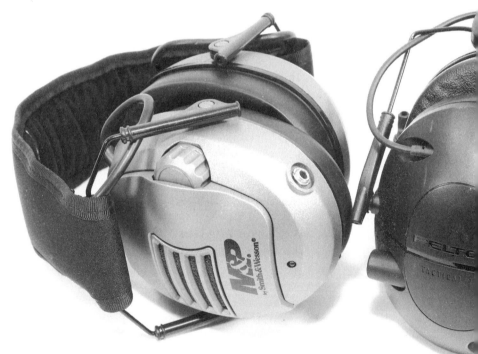

Muffs are good, and they save your hearing, but they aren't as fun as a suppressor. And, you may still need them if someone else on the range doesn't have a suppressor on their firearm.

continue to emit visible light. But, that uses up the oxygen in the can.

The follow-on shot, if it happens quickly enough after the first, does not have oxygen in the suppressor. Instead, the suppressor is filled with oxygen-depleted gases.

As a result, the first shot will be louder, sometimes noticeably so, than follow-on shots. If you stop and wait and the hot gases in the suppressor escape, exchanged for ambient air, the oxygen is replenished and it starts over again.

The interior design and size of the suppressor has an effect on this, but as with all things there is no free lunch. If you design a suppressor that does not experience a noticeable first-round pop (aka FRP) then it will have an average sound level slightly higher than one with FRP.

Let's describe an example. Consider suppressors A and B, A being designed for quiet, and B designed for no FRP. We measure five shots each, in quick succession. Suppressor A delivers 136 dB, 134, 134, 134 and 134. Average 134.4 dB. Suppressor B delivers 131 dB, 136, 137, 136 and 137. Average 135.4.

If you are depending on a suppressor for its first-shot performance, say, a SEAL taking out a sentry, you want suppressor B, because the one shot you take will be 5 dB quieter than suppressor A would be. The average is slightly in the favor of suppressor A, but once the firefight gets going, a fraction of a dB either way won't make any difference.

Do not get too excited or too focused on FRP performance. If you are going to be shooting one shot every five minutes, and have to be as quiet as possible, sure. But for most of us, the mere fact that we're down in hearing-safe range is plenty good enough.

FRP can also be caused by using a compromised suppressor. A .45 suppressor on a 9mm pistol will create more FRP, because the volume of the suppressor is bigger than it would be in a 9mm suppressor. Ditto a .308 suppressor on a 5.56 rifle.

Some will assert that a monocore design has more FRP, but I have not seen that as a general rule.

Don't sweat it, it isn't a big deal. But sooner or later, if you have a suppressor prone to FRP, someone at the club will notice it and ask, or comment on why you didn't buy "The XYZ suppressor, that doesn't have FRP?"

CHAPTER 5

HOW THEY ARE MADE

• • •

Simply put, a suppressor is a tube with a series of partitions inside that trap the expanding gases and slow their release into the air. This reduces the pressure wave, and thus the noise, the firearm creates.

The full technical explanation involves physics, metallurgy, heat transfer, the chaotic movement of gases under pressure, and we'll skip that.

The design and construction of a suppressor involves baffles welded inside of a tube.

A production facility needs a lot of machines, and they can be as big and complex as the company can afford. A CNC machining station can produce parts so fast it will make your head swim.

Making a suppressor is both easy and difficult. It is easy, in that pretty much anything you put over the end of the muzzle will dampen noise. (Which can, in some instances and designs, be against the law without proper paperwork.) It is difficult in that what you use to dampen noise can degrade accuracy, cause difficulties aiming, and can be inconvenient, messy and just plain ugly.

Suppressor designers and manufacturers work hard to make suppressors easy, convenient, good-looking, not harmful to (actually increasing) accuracy, and all this while significantly reducing noise.

The basic designs of suppressors fall into two camps, and each is either sealed or user-serviceable. User-serviceable is the technical term for "take it apart and clean it." The two camps are baffle stack and monocore.

If you make stuff, you have to measure stuff. If you were to visit your suppressor maker (most keep the doors closed to all) you'd see a test room filled with measuring equipment like this.

BAFFLE STACK

The baffle stack design entails a tube, and inside the tube the manufacturer places a stack of relatively cone-shaped baffles. Back in the early days, there were two versions, the "K" baffle and the "M" baffle. Today, we have more than two, they all work, and the details matter only to those who obsess over fractions of a dB in on-the-range testing. The baffles are machined to have space between them. The spaces they create are the volume into which the gases will expand. The first of these is called the "expansion chamber."

The baffles can have various shapes, as seen in cross-section, and they can also have holes drilled through them to create

A bin of machined baffles, ready for the next step in the manufacturing process.

Once cast or machined and then surface-treated, a baffle stack can be assembled into its tube, ready to be a suppressor.

turbulence in the gas flow. Turbulence increases efficiency and makes a suppressor quieter, although some argue just how much it matters.

The baffles must be kept in place, so they are machined for a snug or tight fit in the tube. The tube is sealed with front and rear caps, trapping the baffle stack inside. The rear cap also contains the mount design, either direct-thread or QD.

On a rimfire or pistol-caliber suppressor, the front and rear caps are threaded so you can take the suppressor apart and clean it. If you do not, it will collect powder residue, lube and bullet material which hardens into an impressive layer. This can build up until the suppressor is only a heavy tube with minimal clearance for the bullet, and no effective baffles left, the baffles now buried under the gunk.

Rifle-caliber suppressors are self-cleaning, and as a result they are not often user-serviceable. They do not need to be, unless the centerfire rifle you shoot uses cast lead bullets. Then, you'd better have a cleanable suppressor on it.

SEALED SUPPRESSOR WELDING

A sealed unit will have, at the very least, the front and end caps welded to the tube. Generally speaking, more welding creates a more durable a suppressor. There are five levels.

One place synthetics can work is as the monocore of a rimfire suppressor. And if the monocore finally wears out? A replacement is not a controlled part, and will cost $20-30.

CAP-WELDED

Here, the front and rear caps are welded on and the baffles are simply pressed into the tube and trapped in place. While the baffles are tightly packed, they are not attached to the tube.

TACK-WELDED

On these (usually older designs), the baffles are stacked outside of the tube, and the edges welded at two or three points on their perimeters, creating a rigid assembly. The welds are then filed/ground flush, and the baffle stack is pressed into the tube, where the caps then are welded on. Alternately, the tube can be drilled at spots along its length where the flanges of the baffles would rest, the baffles inserted, and each hole weld-filled with the baffles in place. As a result, each baffle has two or three welded attachments to the tube, through where the holes had been.

In this example of partial-weld baffle stack design, these welds will have to be ground flush with the baffle skirts before the assembly can be slid into the tube.

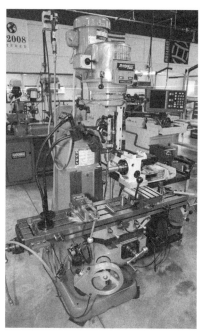

LEFT: And the small, important dimensions? Specialty equipment is required to make sure what you are making meets the dimensions on the blueprints. RIGHT: As a small shop, a suppressor maker might make parts on a machine such as this Bridgeport. The big companies use the Bridgeport to make the parts the CNC machines need to make suppressor parts.

FULLY WELDED STACK

Here, the rim of each baffle is welded its full circumference to the next baffle in the stack. The assembly is then ground or lathe-turned to be round again, and then pressed into the tube, where it can be welded in place or the caps welded on, or both. Also, each can be welded in turn into the tube, but this is a lot more difficult.

FULLY WELDED, NO TUBE

This is the process used by Sig. They fabricate the baffles such that they have external, cylindrical skirts. The baffles are then fully welded into a stack, and the skirts form the tube that the baffle stack would otherwise be shoved into. This is a process that requires a great deal of precise equipment, but the end result is a suppressor with greater internal volume and less weight, since it does not use both a baffle stack and an external tube.

MONOCORE

Here, instead of the baffle stack being composed of a series of cone-shaped parts, it starts as a solid cylinder of the baffle material. Then, through the magic of multi-axis CNC machining, the cylinder has gaps, holes, and baffles machined out of the bar stock of metal. This is then inserted into a tube. The big advantage here is that the monocore can be created in shapes that no baffle stack of cones could ever duplicate.

The monocore tends to be a bit heavier than an equal diameter and length baffle stack, but that can be offset by the choice of tube materials and thickness.

The big advantages are that the extra contours of the monocore can make for a quieter suppressor, and it is easier to make a rifle-caliber suppressor that can be disassembled and cleaned. As a result you can use a monocore suppressor as a multi-caliber compromise, since it is a lot easier to take apart and clean.

There is one other design detail of the monocore that can matter, or not. It is relatively easy to not only make a monocore suppressor that can be taken apart, but also incorporate into the design an external tube that does not have threads on it. The plain tube is the part that

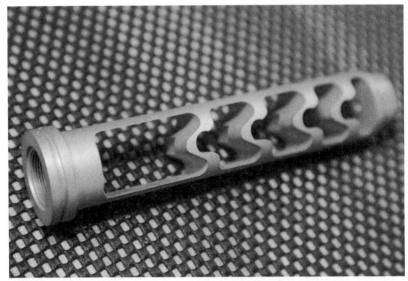

The big advantage of a monocore is the design variation possible in its baffle shapes.

A monocore can have shapes not seen in circular baffles, and if it works, great.

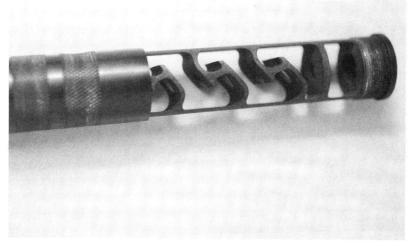

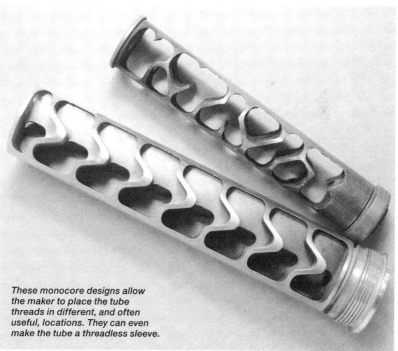

These monocore designs allow the maker to place the tube threads in different, and often useful, locations. They can even make the tube a threadless sleeve.

Machines need operators, and operators need blueprints to work from and compare parts. A good company works hard to attract and keep good people, and the best do.

has the manufactures name, model number and serial number on it. If, in disassembly or cleaning, you were to damage the threads (easy to do if you have neglected it, and it is carbon-welded into a single part), the threaded parts, the front cap, rear cap or monocore can easily be replaced. The tube, lacking threads, is extremely unlikely to be damaged by such heavy-handed treatment, and thus you do not have the headache of having it repaired.

WHICH TYPE THEN?

Which method a manufacturer uses depends in part on when they began making suppressors, how much they are willing to invest in capital equipment, and what the caliber and use demands. A maker that has been in business for a number of years, with familiar equipment capable of making solid, dependable old-style suppressors, may be reluctant (and understandably so) to invest in a lot of new equipment that will make suppressors only a little bit better than what they make already.

As the buyer, you can decide what type you want, with the understanding that the more welding there is, the more it will cost. If you

Very early designs of suppressors had baffles that were simply washers and stamped cones. This worked fine back when cars had fins, but we expect better performance in the 21st century.

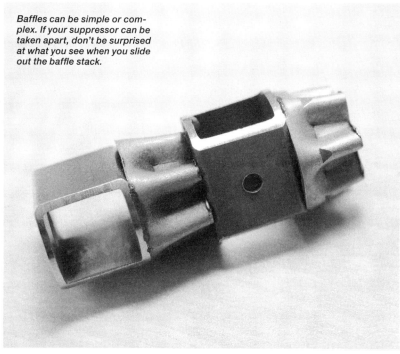

Baffles can be simple or complex. If your suppressor can be taken apart, don't be surprised at what you see when you slide out the baffle stack.

do not need a fully-welded suppressor, then don't buy one. A hunter, for example, really doesn't have a pressing need for a full-auto-rated suppressor. Buying one will entail higher cost and greater weight.

You will be advised by those who claim to be experts that money spent on any suppressor that isn't full-auto-rated, or adopted by So-Com or SEALs or some other black-bag group, is money wasted. You must, simply must, buy the most rugged, extreme-use, manliest suppressor, or you are a poseur, dilettante, or not serious. Ignore them.

This is your decision, your purchase, and you will be the one using it in the future. Buy what fits your needs, your wallet, and your self-image. If that requires weight, exotic materials and a military provenance, go for it. If not, go for it anyway, and have fun.

This modern design uses a monocore, and the tube is a sleeve without any threads on it.

CHAPTER 6

CALIBERS & LIMITATIONS

· · ·

While some suppressors are meant to be "one size fits all," they are compromises. Any given suppressor is designed to handle a given amount of gas, at a specific maximum pressure, and the clearance holes in the baffle stack are meant for a certain caliber and nothing larger.

The two limits should be clear, but it bears repeating. First, you must have a clearance hole down the middle of your baffle stack or monocore that can handle the bullet you are using, or a smaller bullet. That means a .45 can handle .40 and 9mm, and a .40 can handle 9mm. A 9mm can handle only 9mm, unless it is rated for smaller bullets but larger cases. If it is, the manufacturer will tell you.

Then, the suppressor has to be rated for or made for a case of that size or smaller. So, your .308 suppressor will handle a .243, but might not be so long-lasting if used in a .30-06. And it definitely won't like a .300 Win Mag.

Last, you need some way to attach it.

That said, you can use your suppressor on a bunch of different-caliber firearms, but you have to understand the manufacturer's stated limitations. Let's start with a theoretical one size fits all (OSFA, for short) suppressor, and see what we're in for.

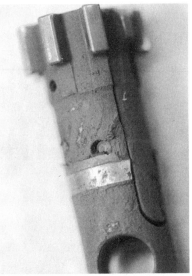

Suppressors increase dwell time, and that blows lots of crud back into the receiver on an AR. This bolt is grubby after an hour's worth of plinking with a suppressor. Lube your firearms, and clean them afterwards.

OSFA

Let's assume the manufacturer puts an upper limit of .300 Winchester Magnum on their OSFA suppressor. That means it will be either a big and heavy stainless steel and Inconel or Stellite design, 10 to 12 inches long, over 20 ounces, and it'll have the added expense of being a take-down design. Or, it is even more expensive, made of titanium, and thus ounces lighter but hundreds of dollars more expensive.

Why? It is big and heavy because it has to handle the uncorking pressure of the .300 Win Mag, where you can be shoveling as much as 80 grains of powder into the case, and not less than 60 grains, to propel your bullet. That's two to three times as much powder as your .223 cartridge uses. It isn't just the uncorking pressure but also the gas volume created by up to 80 grains of slow-burning powder that your suppressor has to deal with.

So, do you really want to have a suppressor that is that long and heavy, on your AR, or your .22LR rifle?

And the take-down part? Well, if it is going to be used on your .22LR, you will have to take it apart and clean it, or you will eventually load it up with powder residue and lead, making it both heavier

A regular-length barrel has a gas port drilled for the dwell time of the rifle. Add a suppressor and you increase dwell time, and thus work the rifle harder. And grubbier.

An SBR has a shorter and less forgiving dwell time. A suppressor can markedly increase the dwell time and the stress put on the rifle.

and louder. Oh, you could follow each .22LR range session with enough big-bore rifle shooting to in essence burn out the gunk, but will you? Really?

One suppressor to quiet them all is a nice idea, but by the time you get done handling all the compromises, you are stuck with a really awkward suppressor for all but the most extreme uses of the compromise set.

The back-up plan to this is a suppressor that doesn't handle them all, but handles enough of them that it is useful for your needs. Here you can make some progress. A compact .308-level suppressor isn't unwieldy on a .223/5.56 and, while a bit heavy and giving up a few potential dBs compared to a .223-specific suppressor, it will work. A lot of people do that.

That's the thing to keep in mind when you are looking at a suppressor that will serve in more than one role: it has to handle the most extreme of the uses it covers, even if that makes it less attractive for the lesser-extreme situations. The wider you cast your net, the less suitable it is for each specific use.

Think of the OSFA suppressor as the four wheel drive truck with extra ground clearance and big-lugged tires. Is it really what you need to drive to the corner store on a sunny Spring afternoon? If your house is four miles from the nearest road, which is itself merely a dirt track, then maybe. For those of us who live with paved roads all the way, obviously not.

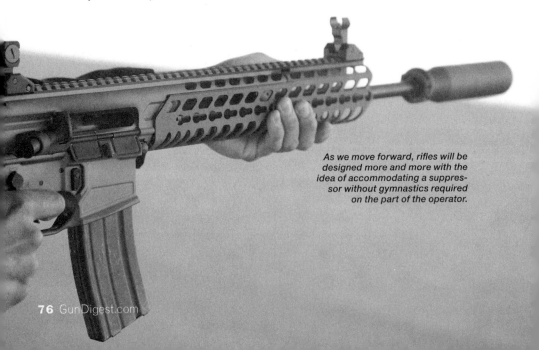

As we move forward, rifles will be designed more and more with the idea of accommodating a suppressor without gymnastics required on the part of the operator.

RIMFIRES

This one is easy. There is the pure .22LR suppressor, the ".22LR and the magnums" version, and a rimfire suppressor that handles .22LR, all the magnums, and the FN 5.7 cartridge as well. The extra cost and weight of the full-spectrum rimfire suppressor isn't that great, so unless you are looking for the absolute lightest suppressor for a .22LR rifle, the extra ounce of weight the full-spectrum costs you is no big deal. The monetary cost may be a bit more, depending on the manufacturer. It can be an extra $50, it might be an extra $150.

The "magnum" here is the .22 Magnum and the various .17 rimfires, not to include the biggest one of all, the .17 Winchester Super Magnum. That one fires a 20-grain bullet at 3,000 fps, which is a lot to ask of a rimfire-intended suppressor built for .22LR. If you really have to have a suppressor on your .17 WSM, you may have a long search ahead of you, and you might just have to settle for a suppressor that is rated for the .223/5.56.

Typically, rimfire suppressors are all aluminum, with some of the more rugged (and expensive) designs using stainless baffles. One, made by Inland, uses a polymer monocore baffle, and when the baffle gets too worn from use and cleaning you simply replace it with a new polymer monocore.

Rimfire suppressors must be disassembled and cleaned on a regular basis.

A compromise here isn't much of one, as you can easily find and buy a suppressor that will handle everything in the rimfire and small-bore arsenal, without being big, heavy or expensive.

HANDGUN ONLY

These are set up and designed for use on a 9mm, .40 or .45 handgun. They are expected to deal with the minimal uncorking pressure that handguns can produce. Yes, the 9mm and .40 operate with a maximum pressure of 36,000 PSI, but few loads reach that as the normal operating pressure. And, at the end of a 5.5- or 6-inch barrel, the uncorking pressure isn't all that great.

The problem with handgun-only suppressors is their weight. When attached to the barrel, the weight of the suppressor can be enough extra that it prevents the pistol from cycling. As a result, manufactur-

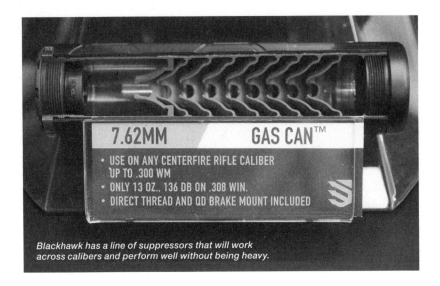

7.62MM   **GAS CAN**™
- USE ON ANY CENTERFIRE RIFLE CALIBER UP TO .300 WM
- ONLY 13 OZ., 136 DB ON .308 WIN.
- DIRECT THREAD AND QD BRAKE MOUNT INCLUDED

Blackhawk has a line of suppressors that will work across calibers and perform well without being heavy.

ers incorporate a special rear cap assembly called a "booster." It stores energy in the start of the recoil cycle, and then feeds it back into the system. As a result, it increases cycling reliability.

It does this with the curious result that a pistol, with the extra weight added, has more recoil than without the suppressor.

The rear caps for 9mm, .40 and .45 have caliber-specific threads, so they cannot be put on the wrong pistol barrel. You can put the larger one on a smaller one (.45 on a .40 and/or 9, and .40 on a 9mm) but you'll need the correct rear cap adapter mount for this conversion.

Also, the common thread pattern for the 9mm pistol use is ½-28, the same as that of the .223/5.56. This would be a bad combo to get mixed up, so if you have friends at the range, watch them closely.

Handgun-only suppressors must be disassembled and cleaned on a regular basis.

HANDGUN AND BLACKOUT

The .300 Blackout offers a low-enough uncorking pressure with some loads that it can be managed by a 9mm suppressor. A multi-use suppressor will be clearly described as to what it will handle. A typical description would be "9mm ammunition and .300 Blackout subsonic." Using .300 Blackout supersonic ammunition will stress the sup-

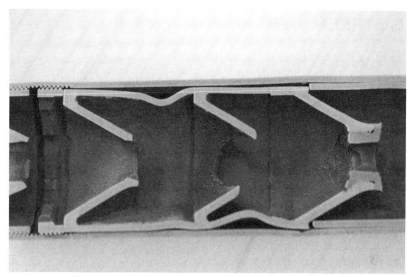

If you abuse your suppressor, it will eventually give up under the load. Not only is the central baffle on this stack worn, but the suppressor was grossly over-heated and the baffle skirts buckled under the work.

pressor beyond its design limits. Another might say "9mm ammunition and all .300 Blackout," so you could use supersonic .300 Blackout in that suppressor.

If you suspect that the second of these is larger or heavier and costs more money, you are probably correct.

Such suppressors must be capable of being disassembled for cleaning, as the 9mm ammunition will dirty them up beyond the capacity of the .300 Blackout to clean them.

CENTERFIRE ONLY, .300 BLACKOUT

This would be a very compact and lightweight .308-based but modified suppressor, with the intention of only being used on .300 Blackout. Since it doesn't have to handle the uncorking pressure or gas volume of a .308 cartridge, it can be made lighter and shorter. That does, however, make it unsuited for 9mm (as above) or .308 use.

It most likely won't be made for disassembly, since it will only ever see jacketed ammunition, and regular use with supersonic ammunition will heat it up enough to burn out whatever residue the subsonic ammunition left in the interior.

CENTERFIRE-ONLY .223/5.56

Here we have the second-most common suppressor (.22LR/rimfire being the most common) and one that is very useful. This will work with all smaller calibers, such as the .204 Ruger, the centerfire .17s, any smaller-case .22 cartridges, and not be big and heavy for them.

You will most likely see such a beast on an AR at the gun club, and it might well live there all the time.

CENTERFIRE .308

This will handle the .308, obviously, but some might be capable of handling a .30-06. They will also handle anything smaller in bullet size but based on the .308 case or close to it – the 6.5 Creedmoor, 6.5 Grendel, .243, .257 Roberts, .260 Remington, you get the idea. It will also handle anything the .223/5.56-rated suppressors will, but at a higher cost in weight, size and expense. Still, a few ounces and a hundred dollars more for a suppressor that will work on both your .308 hunting rifle (or the others noted above) and your AR-15 plinker is not a lot to pay for a not-bad combo.

MAGNUM .300S

This is what you'll need for the .300 Winchester Magnum and above, but also the bigger .308s and smaller-bore big game cartridges. If you have, for example, a 7mm Remington magnum you want to suppress, I would not put a .308-rated suppressor on it. It generates too much gas, and probably is loaded with too-slow-burning a powder for your .308 suppressor to be happy or survive long.

It would work great, however, on our .308. It would be too big for use in a .223/5.56, at least if you expect the assembly to be handy. It

One advantage of using a .30 suppressor on a .223 rifle is that it will be a bit more forgiving of misalignment. Not that you can put one on crooked, but you do have a bit more elbow room.

will suppress shot sounds, but do you really want to add a foot-long suppressor to your AR carbine?

However, if it is what you have and you want to use it until your .223/5.56 suppressor is approved, then go for it.

.338S

This is a specific niche, meant to handle the suppression of a .338 Lapua Magnum. The 338LM is essentially (but not exactly) a necked-down .416 Rigby, and pumped up in operating pressure. It was meant to be a near-.50BMG cartridge, but one that did not punish the shooter as much as a single-shot .50. If you have a suppressor for this, it will work just fine on your .300 magnums, but it will be big for a .300, and absurd on a .308. A .223? Get real.

Any time you use a suppressor on a caliber it is not directly designed or intended for, you also have to deal with the mounting system. If you want to, for instance, put your .308 suppressor on your AR, you have to find an adapter for the threads. Or, if it is a QD system, you'll need a QD mount with .223/5.56 threads and .308 QD socket, which will only be made by the manufacturer of your suppressor. If you want to use a suppressor across systems, do your homework and

No one runs a bolt gun fast enough to work a suppressor very hard. A hunter will work it much less than a tactical competitor.

A piston-driven system can be more forgiving, but better yet, it can be adjusted for use with and without a suppressor.

find out if the prospective maker makes the adapter parts, direct-thread or QD, to do what you need. If they don't, buy something else. If no one does, take that as a hint.

To summarize, you'll need a suppressor with a clearance that bullet diameter or larger than what you will mount it on; a case that is the same size or smaller than the one the suppressor is made for; and a mounting system that can be adapted.

BARREL LENGTH & GAS

One urban myth you will hear is "suppressors increase back pressure." Well, yes and no. They don't increase the pressure, what they

actually do is increase the dwell time. This matters in self-loading rifles.

When the bullet goes past the gas port, it lets gas escape into the gas system. This system is pressurized for as long as the bullet stays in the bore. Once it leaves the muzzle, the gas system drops back to ambient. The rifle designers knew what the dwell time would be, and the pressures of the gases involved at the location of the gas port. They designed it for a certain dwell time, and your suppressor will increase that time.

As a result, a lot of rifles will be over-driven when there is a suppressor mounted. That's the source of the gas coming back in your face. The gas you experience is also influenced by the burning rate of the powder used in your ammo.

Short-barreled rifles are in a particularly bad spot. The dwell time is typically very short. The manufacturer has to provide a large-enough gas port to run the rifle with any factory ammo, both weak and stout. Add a suppressor and the rifle gets really hammered.

This situation is the attraction for two approaches: a piston-driven AR, and adjustable gas blocks or bolt carriers. Both help, neither is perfect, and until we have rifles designed to run either way, you'll have to settle for compromises.

CHAPTER 7

HOW THEY ATTACH

• • •

You can't just use duct tape and baling wire to attach your suppressor to your firearm. Well, you can, but it will be ugly, and temporary, and people will talk about you.

The only solid way to attach a suppressor is with threads on the muzzle. This leads us to the ways to make your firearm suppressed: direct-thread, QD, all of the above, booster and integral.

ABOVE: Gemtech makes their Halo suppressor to mount directly onto an A1 or A2 flash hider. You still need to make sure it is properly aligned, of course.

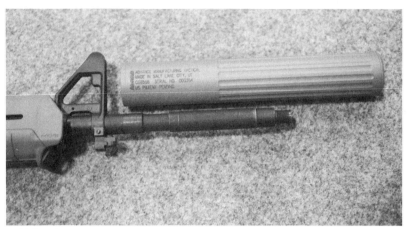

AMTAC makes a line of "reflex" suppressors that fit halfway or two-thirds over the length of your barrel, so they don't add any more length than needed.

DIRECT-THREAD

With direct-thread, the attachment is simple: the muzzle is threaded, the suppressor has the same thread pattern, and you simply screw the suppressor onto the barrel. This is inexpensive, durable, simple and provides a clean attachment. The drawbacks are that it requires a wrench to properly tighten the suppressor or remove it, you are putting that torque into the barrel or action bedding every time you install or remove the suppressor, and it is clumsy to swap a suppressor from one firearm to another.

Torque the barrel or action? Let's say you have a bolt-action hunting rifle you are using as your suppressor host. When you tighten the suppressor, you torque it on with 20 to 30 to 40 in-lbs of force. This force is transferred back to the recoil lug in the action and then the stock. You are putting that force onto the bedding every time you put on or take off the suppressor.

On ARs, that torque will be borne by the narrow little slot in the upper receiver, where the barrel index pin rides. You can use a Geissele reaction rod to take the torque instead of the pin, and you should.

This isn't a big deal most of the time, but what if you leave your suppressor on the rifle for several range trips? Hundreds of rounds? It could be on there "really tight" and you and your buddy have to wrestle with the rifle (unloaded, please) and even whack the wrench handle with hammer in order to loosen the suppressor.

This Poseidon suppressor is so light and compact it can be used on a pistol without a booster, and on a carbine with the right thread insert.

Clumsy swapping comes from the threaded section at the muzzle. An AR-15 barrel will be threaded 1/2-28, as will be .223 bolt-actions threaded for suppressors. If the threaded section is only half an inch long, it will require fourteen turns to install or remove the suppressor. Three-quarters of an inch, and it becomes twenty-one turns. That's a lot of spinning of the suppressor, to get it off one rifle and onto another.

To install or work on them at the range, you need tools. Here is a common crescent wrench and an uncommon PBR (portable barren wrench) from M-guns. With these two, you can change most suppressors at the range.

QUICK DETACH

Quick-detach (QD) mounts are cool. They only require a turn and a half or so, depending on the make and model. They are, however, more expensive than the direct-thread, and add weight to the full-up suppressor as-mounted.

The process involves a special mount, called a "muzzle device," which is a modified flash hider or muzzle brake. This device has on the inside the threads needed to secure it to the barrel. On the outside

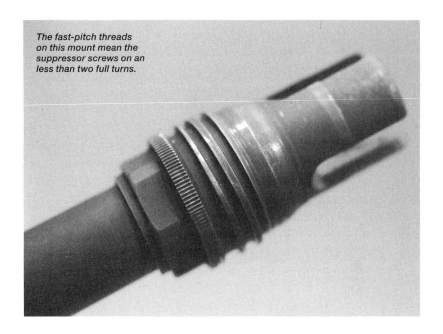

The fast-pitch threads on this mount mean the suppressor screws on an less than two full turns.

it has an indexing surface or two, and the fast-pitch threads to spin the suppressor on in the turn-and-a-half of its design. You attach the device to the barrel more-or-less permanently, with a very strong locking compound, and leave it on the barrel.

You can also attach that muzzle device permanently. You would do this to make a 14.5-inch barrel for an M4 long enough to be a regular carbine (16-inch overall barrel length) and as a suppressor mount. Doing so makes the rifle barrel long enough that it would not be considered a short-barreled rifle (SBR). This only works if the net added length of the mount makes the barrel more than 16 inches long, and if the mount is welded on. If you do this operation and haven't done your arithmetic correctly, the end result is a barrel that is 15-3/4 inches long, so you still have an SBR. Oops.

While cool, QD mounts are also not without problems. First, there is no such thing as a universal mount. Each manufacturer makes its own mount, and no one makes one that will fit some other manufacturers. That may begin to change as some of the big makers start to dominate the market. Let's say, just as an example, that Blackhawk and Sig really gear up for the market and start to sell a significant percentage of all of the 5.56 and 7.62 suppressors made. A small suppres-

With this Sig rifle mount, the left half of the mount is wrenched on and torqued in place with Rocksett. The right half is the muzzle brake, and it is held in position by a crush washer. Clever, solid and easily installed.

sor shop would be smart to offer their product with either or both QD mounts as an option, so that someone who already has such a muzzle device could mount their suppressor as well as one from the big boys.

You can easily swap a QD suppressor from one rifle to another, but to do so requires that both have an attached QD mount, a muzzle device, of the correct type.

This means if you want to use your QD-mount suppressor on three different rifles, they all have to be caliber-compatible, and all three have to have a QD mount on them. That means you have to buy extras, as a QD suppressor typically only comes with one mount.

There will be complaints, there always are. As a friend of mine has been known to say, "Give some people a bar of gold, and they'll complain about the weight." However, this is not a big deal for most of us with most suppressors. The best combination I've run into recently is a Sig SRD556-QD suppressor. The suppressor has an MSRP of $695. The QD mount sells for $60. That means you can buy eleven extra Sig QD mounts before you have reached the cost of your second SRD556-QD suppressor. Do you have an even dozen rifles in 5.56, rifles that you'll be suppressing?

Even if the cost of the QD mount was three times that (and I'm sure

When you use a muzzle brake mount, you have to time it so the brake will diminish recoil, not just change the direction you have to fight.

there's someone out there who lists their QD mount for $180) you can still buy three extra QD mounts (with cash left over) before you reach the price of your second $695 suppressor.

A muzzle device also acts as a flash hider or muzzle brake (one or the other, not both) when the suppressor is off. But it does add weight and complexity.

The best comparison here is again Sig, as they make identical suppressors in 5.56, one direct-thread and one QD. The direct thread is $545, vs. the QD at $695. The direct-thread weighs 11.5 ounces and the QD weighs 14, which does not include the weight of the muzzle device, admittedly only an extra ounce.

If you are going to suppress your one-and-only rifle, then you do not need a QD. Or do you? One extra advantage of the QD system is that you can scrub your rifle's bore with the suppressor off. It is a bad thing to lose a cleaning patch in a suppressor. If you leave it in and it gets in the way of a bullet, your suppressor can be damaged or broken. Many rifle suppressors are not happy about having liquids in them when fired, as the decreased volume greatly increases the interior pressure the suppressor experiences. In the parlance, they are not designed to be shot "wet."

Your suppressor comes with instructions and a tool to take it apart for cleaning (if it is meant to come apart). Read the instructions. Don't lose the tool.

With a QD system, you can take the suppressor off, scrub the bore to your heart's content, then put it back on and everything is fine. With a direct-thread system, you have to take the suppressor off, which we've discussed, clean, then re-install.

ALL OF THE ABOVE

The AOTA approach is simple, but it requires extra steps and extra precision. What the manufacturer does is simple; they make the rear of the suppressor tube a gaping cylinder, threaded to accept whatever mounting system you want.

Here, the rear of the tube is not threaded to go directly onto the muzzle, but is threaded to accept the rear cap which is the mounting system. One such system is the Gemtech Multi-Mount. A pistol-caliber suppressor, the rear of the tube can accept a booster for use on pistols. Or, it can take a direct-thread rear cap so you can put it on a 9mm carbine.

The newest, and the exemplar in this arena, is the Blackhawk! System. They offer (as of this writing) seven suppressors, from .22LR up to .338 Lapua Magnum, and the seven of them have 50-some mounts between them. This gives you the option of not only mounting a given suppressor on one of several different firearms you may own,

When your gunsmith or machinist goes to cut threads on your barrel, make sure he knows to cut them on the center of the bore, not the barrel exterior. Hence the bore spud and dial indicator.

but also of mounting it on different-threaded barrels. How many of the not-common thread patterns Blackhawk! will sell, and how long the situation will last, is difficult to say. But you've got to give them credit for trying.

If you wanted, you could set up a multi-rifle system like this: have a QD mount on the rifle you use most often. Then have the direct-thread rear cap and other rifles that get used less-often. Use the QD rear on the QD mount rifle, and when you want to swap to another rifle, QD the suppressor off. Remove the QD rear cap, and install the direct-thread one. Then thread it right onto the other rifle.

BOOSTER

Booster: not the person who supports the local sports team, but a recoil-enhancing assembly on the back of the suppressor. This is a special part, because only one kind of firearm needs it: a recoil-oper-

This booster assembly is ready to be screwed into the back of a pistol-caliber suppressor. There's a spring in there that will store and release energy to drive the system.

ated pistol. Attaching a 10-ounce suppressor (or heavier) to a 2-ounce barrel when the barrel has to move to initiate the cycle of the firearm is an invitation to not working.

So, the rear assembly of the pistol suppressor, the booster, is a sliding collar, with a stout spring in it. When you fire the pistol, recoil begins the moment the bullet moves. The pistol moves to the rear a measurable distance, before the inertia of the parts is overcome.

When inertia is overcome, the barrel and slide begin to move. But by then, the entire pistol has jolted back in your hand(s). What the booster does is allow the pistol to move back, but the suppressor stays motionless in space, and as a result, the spring in the sliding collar gets compressed. When the recoil can no longer compress the spring, the spring releases that energy by expanding again, delivering the stored energy back into the system.

As a result, a pistol with a suppressor and a booster recoils harder than it would (or at least, feels like it is harder) than the same pistol, lighter by not having the suppressor on it.

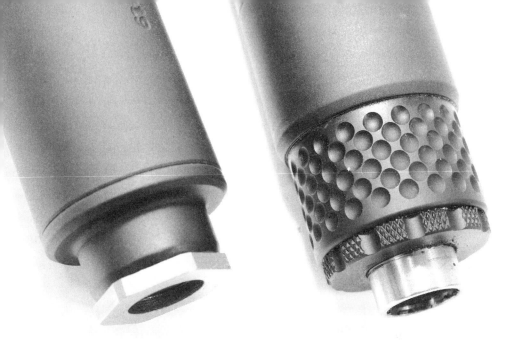

On the left, a plain threaded mount for use on a pistol-caliber carbine. On the right, a booster in the back of a pistol-caliber suppressor, for use on a handgun.

The booster threads and the rigid mount threads for your 9mm (and most of them are 9mm, simply because that's the most-common combo) differ. The rigid mount, which would be on something like a Colt 9mm carbine, will be 1/2-36. The threads on your 9mm pistol will be 1/2-28. But, there will be others, as many European pistols and carbines have different, usually metric, thread patterns on them.

INTEGRAL

Here, there is no mounting system. The barrel and suppressor are made as a single unit, and you install the barrel onto the firearm for use. A classic example is the Ruger 10/22. The barrel is attached to the 10/22 receiver with a clamp and two bolts. It is easy to remove the old and install the new, which is one of the reasons the 10/22 long-ago won the .22 rimfire plinker rifle wars. And pretty much all of the others, until manufacturers realized there were people who wanted ARs chambered in .22LR.

The latest version of this is also from Ruger, and it is an integrally suppressed barrel for the 10/22 Takedown rifle. Here, you don't even have to mess around with wrenches, just remove the t-d barrel from

Integrally suppressed firearms are nothing new. They are just very cool, and if rare and select-fire like this Sterling, fun beyond compare.

The SilencerCo Maxim is an integrally suppressed 9mm pistol. Very cool.

your takedown 10/22, fit the new, integrally suppressed barrel (complete with its own forearm) and have fun.

Integrally suppressed barrels are also available with ARs, where the integral suppressor is used to make the final barrel assembly just over sixteen inches long. This makes it possible to have the shortest-possible carbine, without ending up costing two tax stamps, only one. One because it is a suppressor-equipped rifle, but not two because it isn't also an SBR.

An example here would be the Gemtech Integra.

A rarity is the SilencerCo Maxim, a pistol that is integrally suppressed. So far, they are the only ones doing that.

How you attach your new suppressor isn't as important as knowing that you must have some system to attach it, and you have to decide which. This decision might have to be made when you place your order. In some instances (and with some manufacturers) you can decide when you pick it up, or even change your mind afterwards.

There are more than just threaded fasteners. Some, like these two- and three-lug mounts, offer a quick attach method.

You can adapt many firearms to oddball-mount suppressors. Here, an owner of a three-lug mount suppressor (meant for use on an MP5) has a mount on a pistol that will accept the suppressor.

CHAPTER 8

ATTACHING YOUR NEW SUPPRESSOR

• • •

Let's start with two pieces of advice that I hope you take: buy a Geissele alignment rod in the caliber of your suppressor. That means a 5.56 or a 7.62 rod, or both. The pistol calibers you need not worry about, and the bigger ones, well, no one, not even Geissele, makes a rod for them. And second: read the instructions. No, I'm not kidding, actually read them. They all come with instructions, and while we all joke about deductions to our man-cards for reading them, do you really want to risk it? Risk breaking your new suppressor, I mean?

I'm telling you this before we even begin the process of mounting your suppressor because, while the risk of misalignment might be small, the cost of it will be great if the odds go against you. The Geissele alignment rod will either be the best $60 you ever spent, or the biggest waste of $60 I've ever recommended. Either way, it is only $60, less than the cost of two weeks of over-priced coffee beverages on your way to work.

A bit of background: the bullet leaves the muzzle of your firearm centered on the bore, that is, spinning on the centerline or axis of the bore. Without a suppressor on the end, if the bore happens to not be centered in the steel pipe that is your barrel, that's not a big deal. A lot of rifles have been made over the previous century or more where the bore is kinda-sorta centered and they shoot just fine. The problem comes when you put a suppressor on it.

If the bore is off-center in the tube, but the threads are cut centered on the exterior, and thus they aren't centered on the bore, the bullet might not travel down the center of the baffle stack. If the bullet grazes the baffles, it might not cause problems, but it won't be as accurate as the rifle is without the suppressor attached. And if it hits a baffle hard enough? Ouch. Called a baffle strike, it can range from annoying to catastrophic. Manufacturers have been known to "solve" baffle strike problems by reaming the bore hole down the center to a slightly larger diameter, but that isn't really a fix. What you want is a set of threads on your barrel that are centered on the center of the bore, axial (that is, pointed in exactly the same direction) and with a square shoulder at the rear. If you do not have all three, you will probably not be happy with your new suppressor, and if things are far enough off, your new suppressor may not survive for very long.

The rod won't cure a problem, but it will tell you if there is one, something you cannot do by eye.

The Geissele alignment rod is a precision-ground steel rod, hardened and made to be as straight as possible without insane cost. Yes, you could make it straighter than a thousandth of an inch, but that veers into aerospace standards, and you do not need a NASA-grade alignment rod for your suppressor. Everyone who hears about this wondrous device asks the same question, "Can't you use a regular piece of steel?" I tried, many others have tried. The standard stock sizes of steel rod, in various grades, do not come in a size that works for us. Too big, and it won't fit. Too small, and it won't tell us anything useful. And, the standard grades are not meant to be anything more than "straight enough" for machining purposes.

The Geissele rods are ground to be .002 inch under the nominal bore diameter of the caliber involved. And they are straight to within .001 inch along their length. This means they will slide into any bore, and they will be straight.

The use of the rod is simple; once you have your rifle and suppressor, hand-assemble all the parts (that means a muzzle device also, if you have a QD system) on the unloaded rifle. Do this with the rifle in a vise or other holding fixture, with the barrel horizontal. Then poke the rod down the bore. Let it rest flush with the front cap of the suppressor, and look at where the rod sits in the clearance hole of the front cap. Where it sits determines the future of your rifle/suppressor combination.

ALIGNMENT: PASS OR FAIL

Geissele rates the alignment by a set of pass–fail standards: centered, not centered but not touching, touching, not exiting, and one I call Epic Fail.

The instructions direct you to insert the rod into the barrel from the breech end and see how it fits as it passes out the bore. Some rifles won't allow that, and it is just as easy to poke it in through the muzzle, so that's the way I check.

You want the alignment check to end up with the rod going dead-center through the opening in the front cap.

A little off-center is okay, but once it touches the edge of the front cap, it is a fail and you need to correct the problem or move on to the next firearm.

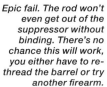

Epic fail. The rod won't even get out of the suppressor without binding. There's no chance this will work, you either have to re-thread the barrel or try another firearm.

CENTERED

When centered, the rod sits perfectly centered in the exit hole of the suppressor. This is what you want, and you will not have any problems with this alignment provided you are using the correct ammunition for your rifle. As an example, even a centered alignment won't help if you have a 1/12 twist and are firing heavy bullets in a .223/5.56 rifle. Those bullets will yaw, and baffle strikes will be a certainty.

NOT CENTERED BUT NOT TOUCHING

Not centered but not touching means you have a less than perfect setup, but you will in all likelihood be just fine. I can't guarantee that, because I don't know how far "not centered" your rod is, and you may find that it works for you. Off a little, maybe barely noticeable?

You're probably just fine, and as good as perfectly centered. Really off-center, and almost touching the front cap hole, but not touching? Hmm, I think I'd fail that one.

NOT CENTERED AND TOUCHING

Not centered and touching the front cap is not good, and you probably should not shoot this combination. There are guys who will, and have done so not knowing this is what their rifle/suppressor combo would gauge. I would not shoot such a combo.

NOT EXITING

This is where the rod stops on a baffle somewhere inside of the tube and won't come out. This is obviously a bad arrangement, and you should not fire it. (Do I really have to tell you that? I hope not.)

EPIC FAIL

I encountered this when I was measuring some AKs for suppressor mounting. The commies hadn't ever considered the muzzle threads for more than a slant brake, and so the threads can be wildly off-center and not aligned. I had some combinations where, having poked the alignment gauge up into the suppressor, it bound in place so tightly that I was worried I'd bend it getting it back out. One suppressor was even visibly tilted on the barrel. I didn't even bother trying to poke the alignment rod into that one.

This should be, as they say in police work, a clue.

WHAT DOES ALL THIS MEAN?

It means that short of an epic fail, a visibly tilted suppressor on our muzzle, there is no way to eyeball the alignment of a suppressor. If you don't have an alignment rod, then you are just guessing. And unlike the lottery, where guessing a set of numbers just risks losing the dollar you put on the counter, guessing wrong about the alignment of your suppressor on a given rifle risks losing you the cost of your suppressor, the tax you paid, and the time spent waiting for it. If someone ever asks, "Can I try your suppressor on my AK?" the answer should be an immediate and emphatic NO.

INSTRUCTIONS

You've all probably worked with mechanical devices before. If you've overhauled an engine for your lawn mower, if you've changed oil, recharged the air conditioner compressor gas in your car, you know that there was a learning curve. You didn't do it right the first time, and sometimes you had to go back and do it over again.

If you make a mistake mounting your suppressor, you may not get a second chance. Putting the right one on incorrectly, or putting the wrong one on an incompatible rifle, will lead to a busted suppressor, perhaps a broken rifle, and maybe even injuries to you or bystanders.

It will only take a few minutes, it may remind you of a step you had forgotten, and the manufacturer might have a slightly different approach to the process, required by their design, a process that you'd never think of.

Read the instructions. Pay attention. Benefit from the mistakes of others.

Read the instructions. This is no time for misplaced manly pride, read the bleeping instructions.

MOUNTING, DIRECT THREAD

Let's assume for the start that your rifle came with a threaded muzzle. In the case of an AR, this usually means there is a flash hider already there. So, remove the flash hider. If it is secured with a thread-locking compound, this may require some wrenching, maybe even an application of heat from a propane torch. Remove the flash hider and any/all washers that might have been used to time the flash hider.

It might be a good idea at this point to recommend you use another Geissele product, their reaction rod. This is a steel bar that engages the locking lug slots in your barrel extension. You use this to put the torque of wrenching off the flash hider into the barrel extension and reaction rod. Otherwise, the little pin in its slot in the upper receiver takes the gaff. Forcing off a flash hider, you can damage the slot and make your rifle less accurate.

You do not want the old washers, and you must not use them, either the old ones or new ones.

This is an important detail that will hold for all suppressor mounting applications: do not ever use the standard washers that come with, or are used with, flash hiders, muzzle brakes or other doodads on the muzzle. None of them.

With a reaction rod in place, you can remove even really tightly secured flash hiders and other devices.

If you ever do have need of some sort of shim or spacer to get a mount, device or other suppressor gizmo properly timed on the muzzle, you should only use whatever washers that manufacturer supplied. They will be guaranteed flat, something other washers cannot be.

With the flash hider off, clean the threads. You can brush them with a nylon bristle cleaning brush, you can use a wire brush, you can even get out a dental pick and pry the residues out of the threads. But get them clean. It would not be beyond reason, if you have one available,

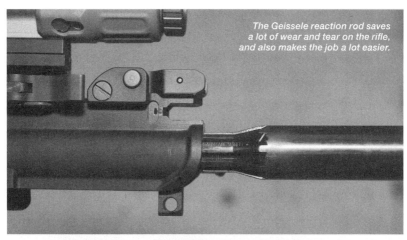

The Geissele reaction rod saves a lot of wear and tear on the rifle, and also makes the job a lot easier.

Use shims as feeler gauges to find out how many you need to correctly time or clock your muzzle brake.

WHY NOT WASHERS?

Washers are not flat, and were never intended to be. The washers you see on your AR-15 are either peel washers or crush washers.

The peel washers are multiple layers of foil-thick metal that have been glued into a plywood-like metal swathe, and then have the final-product washer punched out of the sheet. They are meant to be easy to adjust to a needed thickness by peeling off as many or few of the layers as you need. They are not flat. How can they be, with adhesive slathered in-between layers of foil, and then punched out by a machine that created foil washers?

The crush washers are made as small circular cones, and they act as springs. When you tighten the flash hider down against the crush washer, you compress them and the cone flexes out. It secures the flash hider by two means: it pushes the flash hider forward, increasing the friction on the threads holding it, and the same pressure creates more friction between the washer and the back face of the flash hider. The crush washer is not flat, and it cannot create an even thrust forward, to keep things in line.

And the whole shebang is built up based on 1950s ideas of a flash hider, to hide flash – not be absolutely centered so you can decades later mount a suppressor there.

They are not flat, and they will tilt your suppressor if you use them.

LEFT: Each manufacturer sends their suppressor out with shims, if mounting it will require shims. Use them, and use only them. Do not try to be "economical" and re-use the washers that came out from under the flash hider. RIGHT: If the manufacturer wants the mount to be indexed, or timed, they will say so. And they will include instructions. Read the instructions.

to use a tapping die to chase the threads and make sure they are clean.

While you're at it, also pay attention to the bearing shoulder, the surface at the back of the threads, the one your suppressor is most-likely to stop against. Clean all the gunk off of that surface, also.

Hand-spin your suppressor onto the barrel (you've done all this after making sure the rifle is unloaded, haven't you? Haven't you?). Then insert your Geissele alignment rod. Look at the alignment, and don't kid yourself. What is it, really?

JUDGMENT TIME

This part applies to all suppressor mounting systems and applications. So, when I later in the book say "check alignment," I mean go through this whole process. It thought it would be just a bit pedantic, and per-haps even a bit insulting, to throw all of this next part into each and every section where I put "check alignment," so it is here for all those times. Pay attention, the suppressor you bust may be your own. (And probably will be, when the owner insists you pay for its replacement.)

NO JOY

If it is Fail, or Epic Fail, then you cannot use your suppressor on that rifle. You may only have the one rifle and the one suppressor. I feel for you, but having only one of each is not going to change the results or the future. If you mount that suppressor on that rifle, there will be an unpleasant surprise, and very soon.

Your choices are simple: buy another rifle, replace the barrel on this rifle, or have a gunsmith/machinist re-thread the barrel so it is correct and not too short. This last one won't be much of an option if what you have is a carbine with a 16.1-inch barrel. There really won't be much a gunsmith can do with it. A 20-inch rifle can be trimmed back an inch, re-threaded, and be a one-off rifle. But there aren't many other options.

CAREFUL JOY

If it is off-center but not touching, then you have to decide how much risk you are willing to take. A very slightly off-center but not touching situation is no big deal. But if it is off-center and not touching but almost touching, then the risk increases.

One thing you can try here is remove the suppressor, re-clean the threads and try again. Also, you can use a torque wrench or an open-end wrench and an educated arm to tighten the suppressor to its correct working torque. You might get lucky. You might find that there was some un-noticed bit of grit or left-behind Loctite that caused your suppressor to tilt slightly.

Also, you might find that the bearing shoulder has a slight high point, and when you tighten the suppressor it evens out, straightens up, and your suppressor now passes the test.

In a rare instance, there might be a left-behind tool mark on the bearing shoulder, and carefully stoning this flush removes the suppressor tilt.

JOY, JOY, JOY

Your suppressor tightens on with the alignment rod, centered. Then make sure it is torqued to the correct limit and plan for the next trip to the range.

MOUNTING, MUZZLE DEVICE

The process here involves more steps because you are assembling more gear. As before, remove the old gear and clean the threads. Take the muzzle device (your QD mount for your suppressor) and hand-spin it onto the barrel, making sure it fits and comes to a proper stop.

The muzzle device must come all the way back to the bearing shoulder and tighten down properly, unless (and this is important) the designer intended it to stop on the crown of the barrel and not the bearing shoulder. If yours stops short of the bearing shoulder, you have some problem-solving to do.

First, read the instructions again. Is it supposed to stop on the muzzle? Or the bearing shoulder? Is this the correct-caliber muzzle device?

If everything checks out, spin the device off and take a quick measurement of the length of the threaded portion of your muzzle. Then, phone the manufacturer. Explain the situation, and when they ask, you already know the length of the threaded portion of your barrel.

You can see how small this tube is, but it is plenty for the job. Just be sure and degrease the parts before application.

It may well be in your situation that whoever threaded it didn't know (or did it so long ago, no one knew) the standard length for suppressor mounting. Yours may be too long. You'll have to take it to a gunsmith or machinist who can shorten it, and also check to see that it is correctly centered, before you move on.

Assuming the device threads on properly, attach the suppressor to the hand-tight muzzle device.

Fair warning here: when you attach the suppressor to the hand-tight muzzle device, they may stay attached when you go to remove the suppressor. If this happens, stop. Find a wrench to hold the muzzle device in place while you remove the suppressor, as you proceed to the next step.

With the muzzle device hand-tight and the suppressor correctly mounted on the muzzle device, use the alignment gauge to check clearance. Follow the process above of observing and correcting any problems.

If you have alignment problems, the solutions will be much the same as with the direct-thread mounting process, since you are threading the QD mount onto your barrel.

You must have clean threads and a clean bearing shoulder for the mount or suppressor to tighten up against.

SHIMMY, SHIM, SHIM

Some devices will have to be "timed." If you are using a muzzle device that is also a muzzle brake, you want the ports pointing in the correct directions. Just spinning the device on and locking it in place could be counterproductive. Muzzle brakes are meant to counter both rearward and upward motion in recoil. If the ports are pointed wrong, you won't be counteracting those forces, but adding to them. A muzzle device that shoves the muzzle up doesn't exactly help. And one that adds a sideways push to the recoil is not really useful.

The slight problem here is that, once you have mounted the muzzle device, you really want it to be a "pretty much forever" mounting. Or, at least for the life of the barrel. (Suppressors can have a service life of ten times that of the barrel. You will probably be removing this device sometime in the future, to mount the same suppressor and mount on a new barrel on that rifle.)

If you are an accomplished competition shooter, you know how a muzzle brake needs to be timed for you. If not, simply time the brake so the upwards ports are straight up, and you'll be happy.

An additional reason for timing a mount is that the suppressor maker wants the suppressor and mount to be in place with a certain, specific orientation. Surefire is one, and they provide an index wheel

Once you have the correct set of shims ready, degrease everything and get ready to apply the Rocksett or Loctite. Then torque in place and leave it alone for 24 hours or more.

with the suppressor to tell you what shims to use to get the mount in exactly as they intended.

Spin the mount on and look at the ports. Are they pointed up? If you're lucky and they are, move to the next step. If not, you have to shim it. But, you have to use the flat shims the manufacturer pro-vided. As mentioned, Surefire uses a wheel, but the easy way is with a set of feeler gauges and a digital calipers. The mount stops in the wrong spot? Loosen it and align it. Use the feeler gauges to measure the gap. Use the digital calipers to measure an assembly of shims that comes up a thou-sandth thicker than that.

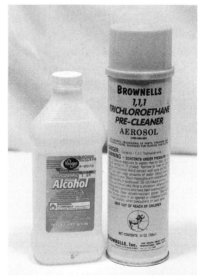

Clean and dry threads before you apply the locking compound and start tighten-ing things.

Remove the mount, slide on the shims and re-install the mount. It should stop at about 10:30 or 11 o'clock on the bar-rel. The rest is your crush/torque turn, to get it up to 12 o'clock.

As a last check, install the sup-pressor and check alignment again. Yes, I'm risking being OCD here, but if something has changed, you want to know before it is all glued together, right?

Before you move on, clear all the rest of the parts, shims, packaging, etc. out of your workspace. It would be a shame, having gone to that work, to fumble, drop the shims you just measured, and jumble them back in with all the others, right?

Scrub the threads clean and degrease everything. Degrease the barrel threads, the shims, the muzzle device and the threads again.

The schmooie you will be using is called Rocksett, and it is an adhesive with some interesting properties. For one, it does not break down at anything close to normal temperatures. The alternative is one of the various grades of Loctite, and those can work well. However, the difference is this: Loctite breaks down (depending on the formula) at 450 degrees, while Rocksett holds at over 2,000.

My personal stash of the best Loctite for many firearms uses: 680 shaft and bearing locker. Fair warning: it sets up quickly, so once you start, don't stop.

Loctite has a higher breaking force level (several to five times stronger) but the temperature is what does it for a lot of people.

The way you remove each is also different. (This is for years in the future, when you are swapping the mount to a new barrel.) Loctite

You can buy a 2-ounce bottle, but most suppressor makers include a small tube with the mount. It is enough to put two or three mounts on rifles, so don't waste it.

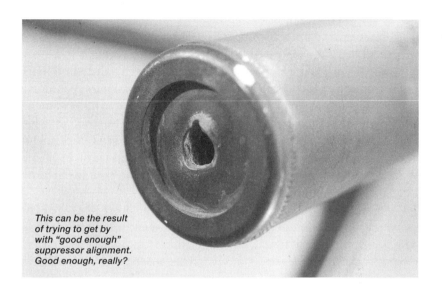

This can be the result of trying to get by with "good enough" suppressor alignment. Good enough, really?

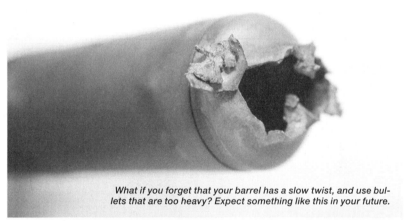

What if you forget that your barrel has a slow twist, and use bullets that are too heavy? Expect something like this in your future.

breaks down at 450 degrees, so you heat it with a propane torch until smoke comes out, and keep it hot (but not over-heating it) until the smoke stops. When it is cool you use a wrench to wrestle the mount off.

Rocksett requires a 24-hour submersion in water, then you wrench it off. Don't worry about the soaking, it isn't enough to cause the mount to rust, and if the barrel is toast, who cares? And rain? Unless you are going to be spending days in the monsoon, or in the rain forest continually drenched, the Rocksett won't be harmed. And if you are in those conditions, you should be worried more about yourself than about the Rocksett in your suppressor mount.

With all the parts degreased, apply Rocksett (or Loctite, if you insist on using it; some suppressor manufacturers do specifically mention it) and use enough to get a full coating without being sloppy. You don't need much, and at $15 for a 2-ounce bottle, you don't want to waste it.

Slide on the shims. Use a clean, small screwdriver to scoop up a bit of the now-dripping Rocksett, and smear it on the outside face of the shims. Thread the muzzle device on, and hand-tighten it in place. Wipe up the excess Rocksett/Loctite, and then use your wrench or torque wrench to tighten the mount in place.

Wipe the area again. When the fluids have not yet set, they are easy to clean up. If you let them harden, you will spend a long time chipping tiny sections of it free.

Now comes the hard part: you wait. Wait at least 24 hours, more is better. Do not "test fit" the suppressor in place, don't shoot without the suppressor, just nothing. Leave it alone for the adhesive to cure, and you will be a lot better off.

ONE EASY WAY

Sig made their muzzle device a lot easier to fit than that. The device, either muzzle brake or flash hider, comes as two threaded-together pieces. Once you have the parts clean and dry, you schmooie up the

AKs are notorious for having off-center, crooked, awful threads on the muzzle. Don't be surprised if your AK fails the alignment gauge, many do.

barrel threads, screw on the muzzle device base, and torque it to spec. Wipe off the excess and let it set. Timing? That comes later. Once the Rocksett or Loctite has cured, place the spring washer on the base, screw on the muzzle brake. Spin the muzzle brake down until it stops. If it is timed, you're done. If not, unscrew it until it is timed, and that's it. The spring washer will keep the muzzle brake aligned, and the brake doesn't touch the suppressor when it is mounted.

Doggone, that's clever.

REMOVAL AND RE-MOUNTING

You may never wear out a barrel, but you may want to swap all the gear over to a new rifle, or one that replaces the one you are selling. As mentioned, removing the mount requires either heat or water. Once you have the mount off, clean the threads. This is where the extra dollars (and not that many of them) you spent on a tap and die set in this thread pattern pays off. Use the tap to clean out the threads on the mount, and the same with the die for the threads on the barrel.

Then, repeat the process above, for this mount system, on the next rifle.

WHAT, NO THREADS?

You want threads on your barrel, and there are none. First, determine the correct thread pattern for the caliber of the rifle you will be suppressing. Second, find a gunsmith or machinist who can do the job. In handing it over, you'll explain what you want, which they will know, but it doesn't hurt for them to know what you want, and that you know it.

The process is simple, if a bit exacting. The gunsmith/machinist will clamp your barrel (or barreled receiver, he will tell you what this machine can handle and you will bring just that to him) in his lathe. The clamping part is called the chuck.

He will place a snug rod into the bore and, turning the chuck by hand, use a dial indicator to read how off-center your bore may be. Here's the interesting and tricky part: he can then adjust the chuck so the rod is running on center, even though it isn't in the center of the barrel. Once the rod is centered, he can then cut the threads, and the threads will be axial to the bore, even though the threads might not be axial to the barrel exterior. When your suppressor or mount goes on, it/they will be centered on the bore. A perfect gauge alignment will be the result.

So, ask the gunsmith/machinist if his lathe has an adjustable chuck on it. If it does not, do not accept assurances that the end result will be "close enough." Close enough might not be, in this instance, even if it would have been for a flash hider or muzzle brake.

CHAPTER 9

TAKEDOWN & CLEANING

• • •

There are two classes of suppressors, and they pretty much overlap the "take apart/ not take apart" designs. The classes are "must clean" and "never clean."

You absolutely must clean your rimfire and pistol-caliber suppressors. As a result, suppressors meant for those applications will always be of a design you can take apart, let's call them MC (must clean) suppressors. Centerfire rifle suppressors may or may not be of the take-apart design. We can call them NC (never clean) suppressors. Why?

Rimfire and pistol-caliber suppressors get really dirty. If you do not clean them, they will become one piece suppressors.

Rifle suppressors (and again, centerfire rifle, not rimfire rifle) run so hot and the powder burns so completely that there is no real residue left behind to clean out. I had a graphic encounter with this while in a suppressor class being taught by Dr. Phil Dater.

There was a rifle-caliber suppressor that had been band-sawed down the center, splitting it into two. Once it had been passed around, Dr. Dater asked us "How many rounds do you think have gone through it?" We hemmed and hawed, and a few numbers were tossed out. In the spirit of full disclosure, there was a hard, thin, coating of powder residue on the inside, but it was about as thick as the brass thickness of the case mouth of an empty piece of brass, not really built-up at all.

I stuck my hand up. "Doc, the way you are suggesting we answer leads me to believe that we're way under the number. So, how about ten to twenty thousand rounds?" With a smile, he said "Closer than anyone usually guesses. That particular silencer had 108,000 logged rounds of .223 and 5.56 through it before we cut it up."

So, even if you take care of your rifle barrel, that suppressor had ten barrels worth of ammunition through it and was still working fine when they cut it open to find out what was going on inside.

At current ammunition prices, that suppressor was good for over $22,000 worth of ammo, at vanilla-plain, FMJ, import ammo prices. (108,000 rounds, at $205 per thousand, although I'd bet if you or-

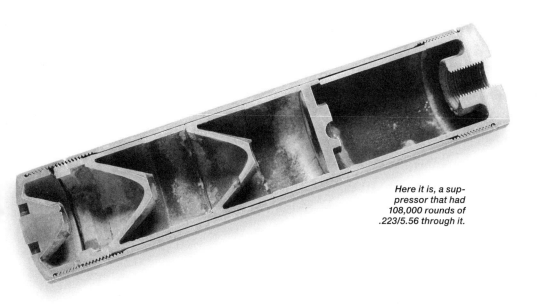

Here it is, a suppressor that had 108,000 rounds of .223/5.56 through it.

dered 100,000 in one delivery, they'd give you a discount.) Twenty-two thousand dollars in ammo for the service life on a suppressor, and you're sweating the cost of an extra QD mount to put on your second rifle? You will literally wear out several barrels each on those rifles before you even have to wonder, "Is my suppressor used up yet?"

So, rimfire and handguns, clean regularly. Centerfire rifles, run them hot at least once in a range session and don't worry about it. (Unless you are reloading cast bullets, for subsonic rounds, and then you treat it like a rimfire or handgun suppressor. And, obviously, do this only with a suppressor you can take apart.)

THE EXCEPTION

There's always an exception. What if, since the threads are the same, you used your centerfire rifle suppressor, meant for .223/5.56, on your rimfire rifle? What then? You will have built up residues inside of the suppressor, residues that cannot be easily cleaned out. One option is to use one of the ultrasonic cleaners (which we'll get to shortly) but then you have liquid left inside. Unless you bake the suppressor to dry it out (and do not, I repeat DO NOT do this in the oven your wife cooks in), the liquid will be adding stress to the suppressor on every shot, until you burn it out. Not good, unless it was designed to be run wet.

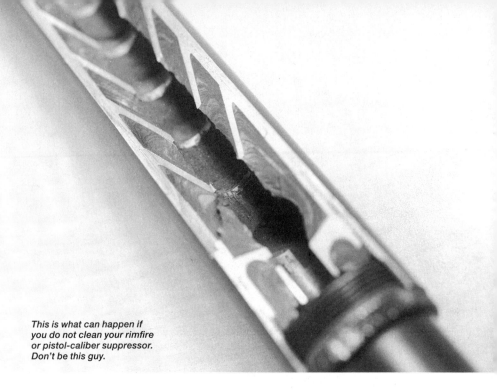

This is what can happen if you do not clean your rimfire or pistol-caliber suppressor. Don't be this guy.

The second way is to take it off the rimfire rifle, put it on a centerfire rifle, and shoot it enough to burn out the residues. Let's take a moment and do the math on that. Let's say you can (and I'm not saying this is the correct number, I'm just using it as an estimate) heat up the suppressor hot enough to clean it in 100 rapid-fire rounds. That's one-tenth of a case of ammo, so $20. That one percent of the service life of the barrel, so there's another couple of bucks there. We'll overlook whether the range, gun club, buddy whose field you are using will be happy at three magazines straight of rapid fire.

How many "cleanings" like that can you do, before you've reached the cost of a rimfire-specific suppressor? Ten? Twenty?

Don't be "that guy" at the range. Restrain yourself, save up the money, get a dedicated rimfire suppressor, one that can be taken apart and cleaned, and then use it on your rimfires.

CLEANING ESSENTIALS

At a bare minimum, you will need a plastic bristle brush, cleaning patches, (I'd suggest a roll of paper towels as well), cleaning solvents for powder and lead residues, and gloves. Gloves? Yes, you will be handling the baffles or monocore directly, and in rimfire and hand-

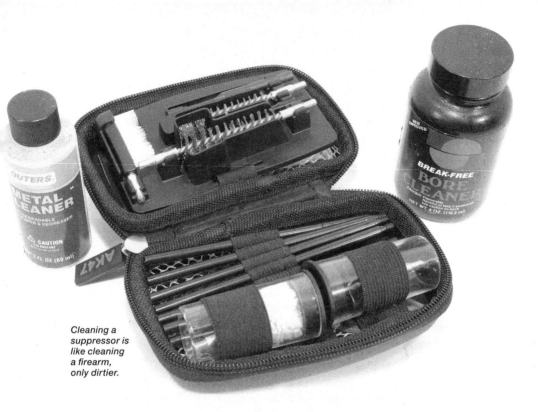

Cleaning a suppressor is like cleaning a firearm, only dirtier.

gun calibers the residues will have a good dollop of lead in them. One might even be tempted to use the pun "a healthy dose" of lead. Keeping that stuff off your hands is a good idea, even if you diligently wash up afterwards, because it will take a lot of washing.

Avoid using brass or steel-bristle brushes, as the baffles might not like it. If you have aluminum or titanium baffles, a stainless steel brush will be entirely too harsh. Finding out the hard way will be expensive.

A cleaning apron specificly for this task is another good idea. The brush will splatter solvent, and your hands and arms will quickly be enveloped in a mist of solvent, with lead and powder residues mixed in. The carbon black of that mixture will stain clothes. (You know how we, other suppressor owners and I, know this, right?)

And it would not be a bad idea to invest in lead-specific soap, for cleaning your hands after you have cleaned your suppressor. You can get some basic soap, or abrasive soap meant specifically for cleaning lead off your hands from D-Lead. If the top of your workbench is not sealed, you should seal it before more solvents, lead and other stuff soaks in. Once sealed (any polyurethane will do, if the top surface is wood), you can use the D-Lead wipes to wipe the lead gunk up when you are done cleaning your suppressor.

Use the tool the maker provided. Get it apart before it gets too dirty. Clean it, and put it together. It isn't rocket science.

TAKEDOWN

Every design is different. Some are threaded on the front cap, some on the rear, some on both. One thing you can be certain of is this: the manufacturer will have either included a special wrench with the suppressor, or designed one or both of the caps to accept a standard open-end wrench. Before you start, make sure you have all the cleaning equipment on hand – solvents, brushes, patches, gloves, etc. – and proceed.

Apply a few drops of penetrating oil to the joints of the front and or rear caps. These could be Kroil, Liquid Wrench, or whatever your favorite loosening liquid might be. While those drops soak in, assemble the tools you'll need.

HAND-CLEANING THE SUPPRESSOR

Use the provided wrench, or an open-end wrench if that is the appropriate tool, and remove the cap or caps. In the case of a baffle stack design, you will probably find the baffles wedged in tightly. Use a section of wooden dowel to push them out. You can find this at the local hardware or big-box store, and you'll probably have to buy a three-foot section of it, for a couple of dollars. Choose one that's a diameter that will fit inside of the tube, not to tight, but not so small it will flew. A dowel 3/4 inch will do for most sizes, but a quick check on yours will let you know what the maximum size yours can take.

Some designs use a common tool, in this case the AR-15 carbine stock wrench, a tool we all have.

You can also use a similarly-sized section of PVC pipe.

While you're there, also pick up a section of doweling, or PVC, that will be a snug but not tight fit down the center hole of the baffles. Don't take the baffle with you, measure the ID of the hole, write it down, and get a dowel at the store.

The way to remove the baffle is not necessarily straightforward. To remove the baffles, place a shop rag or old towel on your workbench or the floor. Place the rod, standing up, on the towel, put the suppressor minus its caps on top of the rod, and grasp the tube. Push the tube down over the rod, pushing the baffles out of the tube. (Some suppressors might be directional, that is, the baffles go out only one way. Again, read the instructions.)

If you try to hold the tube in one hand and push the rod with the other, you end up not pushing the baffles out. When the alignment goes off-center enough, you can hurt yourself as you push one hand into the end of the suppressor tube.

The correct method will cause the baffles to pop up out of the tube and spill out onto the towel/bench/floor.

Gather them up, count them to make sure you have them all, and begin cleaning. How extravagant you wish to be with the cleaning solvent is between you, your wallet, and the space you clean in. You can simply put the baffles in a stainless steel pan, pour in solvent, let them soak, and then start scrubbing and wiping. Get off as much of the caked-on residue as you can from the baffle surfaces, but pay particular attention to the edges. That's where they bind in the tube.

After you've given the baffles a once-over, use the solvent, brush and a piece of paper towel on the inside of the tube. Also scrub the end caps, especially their threads.

Now, go back and give the baffles another wipe with a paper towel damp with whatever cleaning solution you find works best.

Use a dry shop rag or old towel or paper towels to wipe everything dry.

RE-STACKING

Getting all the baffles to stack correctly, and keep them there while you slide them into the tube, can be a hassle. This is especially true if the baffles have index tabs or interlocking edges. This is where your smaller-diameter dowel comes in handy. Assemble the baffle stack over the dowel, keeping the tabs in their slots. Then, you can hold the

This stack of baffles on the rod is ready to go into the tube.

assembly all in one stack, and slide the stack, with the dowel, into the tube. Once in place, with everything nestled correctly, you can pull the dowel out and screw on the caps.

On re-assembly, put a drop of oil on the threads of the end caps, before you screw everything back together.

Tighten to the manufactures specs (you did read the manual, right?) but not tighter. The powder residue and gunk will act to tighten the assembly once you do some shooting, and if you over-tighten you'll simply make it that much harder to take apart when it comes time to clean again.

If you aren't sure if you have it tight enough, don't make it tighter. When you next shoot at the range, test the tightness of the caps after a couple of magazines of shooting. If anything is loose, you need to be a bit firmer the next time. If they are all tight, you have done it right.

Surefire makes a rimfire suppressor that comes with an assembly tool. The rod aligns the baffles for insertion into the tube.

ULTRASONICS

Ultrasonic cleaning works via sound waves created in the solution that act to loosen whatever is sticking. When they were new, they were fabulously expensive, thousands of dollars for even the smallest unit, and thus available only to law enforcement agencies and the government. As with so many things, the technology became less expensive and now the rest of us can afford them.

You've got two choices here. You can opt for an ultrasonic cleaner just big enough for the baffles or monocore and tube, or you can get a bigger one. The smaller ones only run $100 or so, and are big enough for rifle bolts, handgun slides and all but the biggest suppressor tubes. The units that can hold a complete AR-15 upper with a 16-inch barrel (none will hold a 20-inch barrel) run on the order of $500. The advantage of the bigger unit is that you can clean several suppressors at once (keep the parts separate) and you can also use the ultrasonic cleaner to clean the rifle upper you used with the suppressor. Suppressed ARs get quite dirty on the inside, and an ultrasonic cleaner is a real boon for cleaning them.

The ultrasonic method will clean things faster most of the time (results vary, depending on how much gunk, how hard it is, etc.), and will do so with a lot less hassle and mess. But, you have to do your homework.

The cleaning solutions made for use in ultrasonic cleaners are not just water with a squirt of detergent in them. They can be (and most are) formulated specifically for particular cleaning tasks. Make sure, for instance, that you do not use ultrasonic cleaner, with the solution to scour steel parts clean, with your aluminum baffles. They might do fine, they might not. Follow the manufacturer's guidelines when it comes to solutions.

The cleaning time will vary depending on the muscle of the particular ultrasonic cleaner you purchased, the solution used (don't mix brands, using machine "X" with cleaning solution formulated for machine brand "Y," for example) and how much of what type gunk has accumulated on your suppressor parts.

Also, do not be fooled. Ultrasonics loosen material, but they do not wipe it off. Oh, some will come off into the solution, making it look pretty nasty after a few cleanings. But you still have to put on gloves and wipe off the loosened, softened gunk.

This complex-looking front cap design actually incorporates the tool sockets for disassembly. Use the tool, don't use a pipe wrench.

Disassemble the suppressor, place the parts in the tray. Pour in solution until the parts are covered, close the lid, turn on the unit and set the timer. When it is done, pull a part out (gloves!) and give it a test-wipe. If the gunk wipes off easily, then wipe the rest and move on. If not, put that part back in, set more time and run it again.

Once you can wipe the residues off, do so, wipe the parts dry,and re-assemble as above.

CLEANUP

The ultrasonic solution will be pretty grubby by the time you are done. The way to extend its use is to have a second bottle for the used solution. Let the solution cool (if you heated it) and the residues settle.

Get your "used" bottle and decant the solution into it, pouring off the liquid gently so you don't also pour out the sludge at the bottom. You can get a reasonably clean used solution that you can then re-use.

With care, you get almost all of the solution in the used bottle, and a thick sludge remaining in the machine. Pour the sludge into a "sludge" container, and set it aside.

When you next clean, use the used solution and top off with new solution to get enough liquid to cover your parts. Decant again into the used container, and repeat.

When the "sludge" container gets full, you have to make a decision. If your municipality or other government area has a way to handle

How much ammo are you really going to be shooting in one session? Clean your rimfire or pistol-caliber suppressor after each range session, and you'll be a lot happier.

toxic waste, such as the jug of lead-laced aqueous solution you now have, great. Hand it over to them, and get another empty container. If not, check with them for recommended or required disposal method in your area.

The shop rags or used, old, towels you've been working on? If you feel you must wash them to re-use them instead of replacing them, here are a couple of tips. Pre-soak them with an aggressive pre-cleaning solution. Use a lot of it. Run them in the washing machine by themselves, and NOT with other cloth articles. Once they are out, clean the washer by running a heavy-duty wash cycle or a sterilize cycle with the machine empty of clothing.

Consider just tossing the shop rags and buying new, since they cost all of 25 to 50 cents each in bulk. You'll spend that much on soap, cleaner, water and machine service life just washing the ones you used.

THE COST OF NOT

If you do not clean your rimfire or pistol suppressor, then what? Unlike the rifle suppressor, the rimfire and pistol models do not get hot enough to burn out the residue. Worse yet, rimfires and pistol rounds produce much larger amounts of residue, relatively speaking, than do centerfire rifle cartridges. It is entirely possible to "carbon weld" your suppressor so it cannot be disassembled. If you get to this point, repeated sessions of penetrating oil, alternated with ultrasonic cleaning, might get it apart. And, they might not.

If you let things get too far, even that won't help. In the class Dr. Dater taught, he had sectioned pistol-caliber suppressors that had never been cleaned. They were essentially powder residue-choked tubes, with locked-in-place baffles, and were noticeably heavier than the clean ones. They were also measurably, but not always noticeably, louder than the clean ones.

Learn from the mistakes of others, do not let your easily-cleaned suppressors get too dirty, and find yourself with heavy, loud tubes.

Unless you have top-grade firearm, ammo and shooter, the accuracy increase a suppressor can provide might not be noticeable. This is good, but not quite good enough to start showing.

THOMPSON MACHINE ISIS22

Instructions for Use and Care

Congratulations on the Purchase of your Thompson Machine Sound Suppressor!
Please read this instruction sheet carefully and completely before shooting your Isis22.

PLEASE MAKE SURE THAT YOUR HOST FIREARM IS UNLOADED, THE SAFETY IS ON, AND THE BOLT/SLIDE IS OPEN PRIOR TO INSTALLING, REMOVING, OR CLEANING YOUR SUPPRESSOR!!

Tips

1. The Isis22 is designed to be quickly and easily disassembled and cleaned by the end user at regular intervals (we recommend cleaning at least every 100-150 rounds). **THIS REGULAR CLEANING IS NECESSARY** to ensure that your suppressor does not become locked together by lead and carbon buildup. It is a good practice to treat your suppressor just like your other firearms and **CLEAN AND LUBRICATE IT WITH A GOOD GUN OIL** promptly after each shooting session.

CHAPTER 10

ACCURACY MATTERS

• • •

One fear that some shooters have is that a suppressor will adversely affect accuracy – that the point of impact will shift, or groups will open up, or both. While that can happen, it is unusual, and it is often not a problem at all. First, why and how?

A suppressor works by slowing down the gases as they leave the muzzle, and thus making them cooler and quieter. However, the first jet of gas is faster than the bullet. Even a fast rifle bullet leaves the muzzle below 4,000 fps, and often much below that. The jet of gas leaving the muzzle when the bullet uncorks has an initial velocity close to 5,000 feet per second. So the first chamber, the expansion chamber, often fills with gas before the bullet has crossed it. After that, the bullet is going through the relatively calm air in the rest of the suppressor.

If the expansion chamber has wonky dimensions or angles that deflect the gases back towards the bullet, they can ever so slightly disrupt it and affect accuracy. However, those details have been well worked out over the last couple of decades,

When you go up to big-bore handguns, the variables the shooter brings overwhelm any effect a suppressor can have. Don't worry, the chances your suppressor harming accuracy are slim to none.

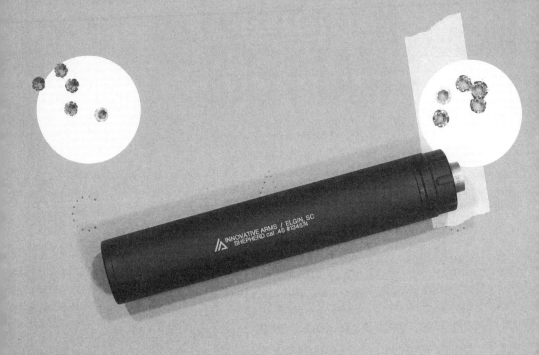

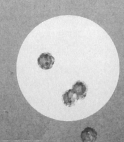

and such bad sizing is unlikely to still be made.

The next issue is harmonics. When you fire a shot, your barrel whips around from the forces acting on it and rings like a bell. If it whips and rings in a consistent manner, then your rifle is accurate. If it does not, your rifle is not accurate. Some of you might remember the Browning BOSS system, from some years back. It was a movable muzzle weight (and muzzle brake, in some models) that you could tune. By adjusting its location on the muzzle, you could adjust the barrel harmonics, and improve accuracy, once you found the sweet spot.

A suppressor can add or subtract from those harmonics, and the sweet spot. Typically, they don't seem to make much difference at all. I attribute this to simple engineering process known as "test and reject". A potential suppressor design that caused accuracy problems would have been junked by the maker, and the ones that didn't, well, they went into production. No need for expensive computer modeling, just a willingness on the makers part to test and accept the results. And scrap the rejects.

What most shooters notice is no change. This is, in part, due as much to the average shooter, ammunition and rifle not being as accurate as we'd all like. It is a personally-held idea, an attribute of the American shooter, that we are all descended from the sharpshooters of the past, and that we all, as a birthright, can buy accurate rifles over the counter.

The accepted standard is "one MOA." That is, one minute of angle or, roughly, one inch at 100 yards. Realistically, it is not an overwhelming percentage of shooters who can do that with any rifle. And while there are more and more rifles capable of it, the combination is what counts. You need a shooter, rifle and ammunition that are all capable of 1 MOA accuracy before you can consistently see 1-inch groups. And for most shooters, that means only from the bench.

The military acceptance of an M16 or M4 is around 3 MOA. They use a very different measuring system, and they are accepting rifles in the ten thousand rifle lot, and ammunition in ten million round lots or more. A rifle that "only" shoots 3 MOA still delivers a 9-inch group at 300 yards, and that is a solid hit on a bad guy.

Most ARs will do 2 MOA, fed good ammo. That's not including the ones built with premium barrels. Most ammo is good for 1 to 2 MOA, so you are right there at the 3 MOA mark. If you use the best

This is an example of the barrel threads causing a problem. There was one last layer of peel washer still stuck to the barrel when the suppressor was mounted for the top rod. Take the suppressor off for the center target. Then clean thoroughly and re-install the suppressor for the bottom row.

ammo, in a premium barrel, put an expensive scope on the rifle, and shoot from a solid bench, it then depends on the shooter. Are you a 1 MOA shooter?

The "half-MOA" shooters at your club typically have one target they can show and brag about. For most shooters, from the not-solid benches and makeshift shooting supports they have, 2 MOA is good, and 3 MOA is normal. Let's do a quick test. Hold out your hand, palm towards you. Your palm is perhaps 3 MOA. Can you shoot a palm-sized or smaller group, at 100 yards, consistently? Look, it's just us, be honest.

So then, what if a suppressor caused a half-MOA shift in the point of impact when it is on your rifle? A half an inch of shift on a 3-inch circle at 100 yards? Can you see that, except standing at the target? Let's say on a good day you can shoot 2 MOA, and on a bad day 3 MOA. If the suppressor opens up your groups half an MOA on average, would you notice?

All of that is to explain why most shooters don't see a change when there can actually be a change. And, there can also be an improvement. I've had the chance to shoot some really accurate rifles, with powerful and precise scopes, using really good ammunition. As in, combinations that can consistently deliver or come close to half an MOA. I'm not a benchrest shooter, nor a High Power shooter, but I have busted enough caps to know how the process of shooting small groups goes. And what I have found is this: most suppressors, if they create a change in the point of impact, do so for less than half an inch at 100 yards. And a lot of the time, that half-inch change is to the good, a half-inch of shrinkage of the overall size, not a shift in location.

Now, if you are a thousand-yard shooter, half an inch at 100 becomes five inches at 1,000. If that matters to you, you are a better shooter than I am, and you probably also have a handle on what you need to do in order to deal with it. My suggestion: when you find a suppressor you like, stick with it, leave it on the rifle, and adjust your zero to correct the point of impact.

For the rest of us, that half-inch isn't something to worry about.

I have also noticed that, if anything, suppressors tend to improve accuracy, they decrease group size. I've had 1 MOA rifles start shooting .75 to .50-inch groups at 100 yards with a suppressor on them.

Back to the moment when the bullet leaves the muzzle.

The reason is simple, if you think about it. When you shove a bullet down the bore, you are spinning it around its center of form, its shape. Once it leaves the muzzle it then has to adjust, changing over to spinning around its center of mass. The better the bullet, the closer its center of form and its center of mass will be to each other, and the less time it spends "settling down."

The technical term for the wobble until it settles down is yaw. Yaw begins the moment it leaves the muzzle, and can take a number of feet to happen. It's happening inside the suppressor.

Without the suppressor, the jet of gases leaving the muzzle create a chaotic cloud of hot gases ahead of the bullet, a cloud that the bullet has to travel through. This chaotic gas cloud can accentuate the yaw and harm accuracy. The suppressor, by stripping away those gases, decreases both the time spent in and amount of gases the bullet is subjected to, in its initial flight.

By stripping those gases, suppressors can have a small but measurable effect to improve accuracy. But, everything has to be small enough that the suppressor effect can be measurable.

A 3 MOA combination of rifle, ammo and shooter isn't going to notice a .25 to .50 MOA improvement in accuracy.

To give this chapter a short summary, any change you see will be small, most likely it will be an improvement, and unless you are a really good shot, you won't notice any change at all.

CHAPTER 11

RANGE ETIQUETTE

. . .

You'd think "This is cool, and quiet. No one can have cause for complaint when I bring my suppressor to the range." You'd be wrong. The mystery and myth around suppressors clings tightly in some circles. If your gun club is (as an example, not to pick on these people in particular) a skeet and trap club, with a small 25 yard range for member's use with handguns and a 100 yard range for them to sight in their deer rifles, you are likely to find yourself getting a cool reception if you show up unannounced with a suppressed rifle.

You'd think every range would welcome suppressors, but that might not be the case. Make sure they're allowed before you show up, or you may be shooting without it for the day.

Even worse if it is a suppressed AR–15.

So, step one is to find out the rules of the range you are going to. If they are online, great, read them. If you are a member and can't remember anyone ever mentioning suppressors, then you have some work ahead of you. If the gun club has not had someone show up to shoot with a suppressor before, the rules might not even cover it. In any case, it may well be up to the individual range officer there that day to say yes or no. If it is a state range, run by the DNR, anything new has to be approved by headquarters, and if they don't have a policy when you arrive, you may have to come back when they do have a policy, or at least shoot that day without using your suppressor, and find out what the answer (and new rule) before your next trip.

Yes, these questions may well have all been answered before you show up, but there's always someone who is first. If that person is you, you may not get to use your suppressor that day.

If it is a commercial range, phone them and ask.

Step two is when you arrive. If it is a commercial range, mention to the counter clerk when you sign in for a lane that you have a suppressor. They'll probably be more interested in what ammunition you'll be using, or telling you that you have to use range ammo, and range ammo only.

On a state range or at a private club as a member or guest, if there is a range officer running that range, mention to them when you arrive that you have a suppressor, and ask if they have any requests of you.

Why all this? Because there are still ranges with restrictive use rules. One round at a time in the firearm is an example, so you can't load up your magazines. They might have had a bad experience with someone who was an absolute pain in the neck, who happened to have a suppressor, and as a result they've been soured on suppressors. You might have to change their minds. You'll have a better chance of doing that if you are polite, and not so much if you are loud and insistent. "These are legal in this state, I went through nine months of waiting to own it, and you're telling me I can't use it?" That approach probably won't help.

Even though you're quieter than the other shooters, you still have to follow safety rules and caliber restrictions, if any, on a given range. The only thing different is that you are quieter.

If the commercial range insists you use range ammo and not your own, you have to decide. Is their ammo good enough to run through my expensive, hard-to-repair or replace suppressor? You might have to establish your good-guy credentials with the range beforehand, so you can get the range equivalent of a papal dispensation to use your ammo and not the range ammo.

OTHER SHOOTERS

Until suppressors become common items on the firing line, using one at the range will get you noticed. Other shooters will stop what they are doing, come over and ask questions. Be polite, they may have only ever seen them in movies, and the only things they "know" about them are the urban myths that "everyone knows." When you get the third degree, it is because they are curious. "Are those things even legal? How much did it cost? How long did it take to get? How much does it cut down the noise? Can I try it? Can I put it on my gun?"

The answers are up to you. You can be specific on cost, or general.

A grand total of four hits outside of the "X" box. A good day, and a fun one, shooting a suppressor and not being abused by the muzzle blast of an SBR. And yes, I let others try it. They had fun, too.

"This one ran $500, but they can range from that up to $1,500." The time is one everyone wants to know, especially those who have already put in their application. So, if it took you five or six or nine months, be prepared to tell exactly how long it took.

As far as the noise level, you'd be well-served to remember exactly what the manufacturer says and be able to recite it. "They give an average number of 36 dB reduction, with military-spec 5.56, on a sixteen-inch carbine barrel" makes people happy. "Real quiet" usually doesn't.

"Can I try it" is usually an easy one. If you're willing, hand them the firearm and a magazine with a few rounds in it. Nobody expects you to hand over a full magazine's worth of ammo, and the smile they get after shooting a few rounds is worth the small cost in ammo.

As for letting them put it on their firearm, there are a couple of good reasons the answer is "no."

It doesn't often come up, as most people do not have a firearm in the same caliber, with a threaded barrel, with the tools to remove flash hiders and a wrench to undo yours and move it over. Especially if you are using a rifle-caliber suppressor with a QD mount, the odds they will have the same mount that your suppressor requires are miniscule.

And, unless you have an alignment rod handy, you can't be sure your suppressor on their firearm will be lined up and safe to shoot. So, the answer is always "no."

THE FUTURE

As suppressors become more common, you will find fewer of these obstacles. And, if you have purchased your suppressor at the new generation of gun shops, no problem at all.

Back in the day, a gun shop was a place to buy guns and ammo. Usually run and owned by a crusty old guy who had opinions on everything, there was typically no shooting there. Ranges were other places. Ranges were often either outdoor ranges run by the DNR or private gun clubs with a particular focus. Some were skeet and trap, others rifle, handguns, competition, hunting, etc. Indoor ranges were there because the weather was sometimes bad, or the city just hadn't moved them out yet. They were usually dim, dirty, smoky, unappealing places, and they sometimes sold guns, but often just sold ammo.

You bought your guns, and had a good time talking guns, at the gun shop. You subjected yourself, in the bad weather months, to the mess of the indoor range. And when the weather was good, you shot outdoors, but only places where you knew they were friendly about your kinds of firearms.

Now, a gun shop is more like a shopping emporium that has a gun club attached. Ranges are light and airy, with video screens, memberships and training available; you can buy guns ammo, gear, clothing and suppressors; and you can check your social media outlets on the free high-speed Wi-Fi.

That place won't have any problems with your suppressor.

CHAPTER 12

THE BUYING PROCESS

• • •

This is not a purchase like any other you have engaged in. In all other kinds of purchases, you look for what you want, and when you find it you conduct the transaction and take home the new thing. The purchase of a suppressor is different. It will be until (and if) the Hearing Protection Act happens.

The current process (at the time of this writing) is a request to the government, specifically to the ATF (the Bureau of Alcohol, Tobacco, Firearms and Explosives) that you, specifically, purchase a specific suppressor, by make, model and serial number, from a specific dealer who is licensed in such transactions. This particular transaction is being scrutinized.

First, you have to find a licensed dealer. Then, you have to find the specific make and model you want and find one that is available. You then pay for it, even though you won't be able to own it for months. And you aren't done yet. Let's go through the steps blow-by-blow.

A DEALER

To deal in firearms, you must have a Federal Firearms License, an FFL. To sell suppressors, you also have to be what is known as a "Special Occupational Taxpayer" or SOT. Back in the old days, this was known in the vernacular as being a "Class Three Dealer." Today, you're just an up-with-the-times gun dealer who can also sell suppressors. (They can also sell machine guns, but that is such a small, specialized market, that few do. The volume is in suppressors these days.) What it means is that the FFL holder who is also an SOT can deal in suppressors and other items covered under the National Firearms Act of 1934, or NFA. Yes, the law we are dealing with is that old, with some extra aspects added by the Gun Control Act of 1968, or GCA.

A lot of buyers go about finding an FFL/SOT backwards, which works. If you already know what make and model suppressor you want, ask the maker for a list of dealers who sell their products in your area. Then thank them and get to the dealer, because the manufacturer can't do anything else for you besides answer questions.

Go to the dealer and have a good long talk with them. You want the XYZ by the Megablaster Corp, do they have one? If they do, great. If they don't, then they can contact the manufacturer and find out if one is available and when it can be shipped. This is necessary because you need a serial number for the paperwork process. If the dealer has one there, then they can tell you the serial number. If not, then the manufacturer can tell the dealer what serial number is available. When you say "yes" and put down good-faith money, they will reserve that serial numbered item for you, and it's yours when the drama is all over.

Oh, and even though you will not be able to take your suppressor home for months (you won't even be able to use it at the gun store, even if they have an on-site indoor range), you will have to pay for it now. You will usually pay for it in full, unless you've already gone through this process. Then, the dealer may (and it is a definite may, it is his/her choice) let you only put down a deposit.

Why? Once that particular suppressor, by serial number, is in-process to you, it is no longer available to be purchased by anyone else. As far as the dealer's inventory is concerned, it is sold and no longer available. Since he can't sell it to anyone else, he might as well insist (and his accountant will insist, if no one else will) that he get paid, up front, in full, right now. You really can't blame him.

He will also have to replace that inventory (if he carries an inventory) and what you pay him goes to buy a replacement suppressor for the stock room.

This long inventory replacement process is why a lot of dealers do not keep inventory in stock, but go to the manufacturer when you request one. A suppressor is a $500 to $1,500 inventory item that has to be financed over a long period of time. Even if it sells the day it arrives, it will sit in the store for six months or more. If it doesn't sell on day one, that is just more time it is in inventory. Welcome to the world of NFA.

The Form 4 on two pages? Not allowed, but just fine for practice and making sure you know all the answers correctly. Print it, try it, be ready for when you go to your dealer.

THE PAPERWORK

You'll need a fistful of forms, a clean background, a valid check and patience. There is also a visit to the local police department, sheriff's office or other place that can fingerprint you. Your dealer will walk you through the process, but knowing what is coming will make it a bit easier for both of you.

You will need three copies of the ATF Form 4, which they refer to as Form 5320.4. Note that, if you print them out from an online source, you must print them back-to-back. You cannot print the two pages of the form on two separate sheets of paper and staple them together. The dealer knows this, but if you have tried to be helpful and have already printed them out, know it has to be printed back-to-back. Even though the dealer will have the forms there, printing it and doing a practice run at home filling it out will help.

Two FBI fingerprint cards are also required. The dealer might have these. If he does not, the police department or sheriff's office will. There may be state or other cards, but the only ones ATF will handle are the FBI cards. Depending on where you are, there may be a charge.

Get fingerprinted.

Then, fill out the Form 4s in triplicate. Mail two of them, along with the FBI cards and a check for $200, to the ATF branch listed on the forms. The third copy gets sent to your Chief Law Enforcement Officer, to inform them that you have applied for this transfer.

Before 2016, you had to submit the forms to the CLEO for approval. This was in the 1934 law, and a holdover from when there was no national database. The legislators back then reasoned that if there was some reason you shouldn't own a suppressor, the local police would know. So, you had to get his or her signature. If the local Chief of Police didn't want to sign, you couldn't make him, which lead to two interesting branches in this process.

One was "Chief Law Enforcement Officer." The Chief won't sign? Go to the Sheriff. The Sheriff won't sign? Go to the Chief. Of course, you had to live where both had jurisdiction. And, the CLEO was defined by state law in many places. So, in some places you could get it signed by the Coroner, the District Attorney or others.

The other option was to form a legal trust, a subject we'll get into in a bit. The trust option was altered by the ATF in 2016, and as a result

The paperwork isn't that involved, but the process is unforgiving. So follow the guidance of the dealer to make sure you have all the t's crossed and i's dotted. (Literally.)

you no longer need a CLEO signature. They no longer have the veto power, they are simply being informed of your application.

Oh, one more important detail: make sure the check will clear the bank. The ATF will deposit it within a few weeks (or less) of your application arriving. Someone will get to the application itself in six months or so. Don't get excited when the check clears the bank, it just means they've deposited the check. Your application is now in the stack with all the others that arrived that day, waiting its turn.

OH FABULOUS DAY

Your approved transfer returns in the mail. You take the approved form, now known as a "Tax Stamp," back to the dealer, where you fill out a Form 4473, just like you would with any other firearm. Yes, that's right, under federal regulations what you own is a firearm because, well, there's no other box on the form to check.

The approved form is your proof of ownership and a tax document. Store it safely, do not lose it, and do not let it out of your possession. Make copies.

What if your application isn't approved?

Chapter 12: The Buying Process **145**

That depends on why. If they have some difficulty figuring out who you are, because there are seventeen illegal aliens using your identity, they may have an agent stop by and talk with you face-to-face, just to make sure you are you and not one of them. If, on the other hand, the conviction you forgot about from 25 years ago that put you on the list of "He can't own a gun" came up in a search, they can't transfer your suppressor. And, they won't refund your money. And, they might just inform the local authorities about the guns you possess.

In the event of a denial, it becomes vitally important to hire an attorney to straighten out the mess created by the traffic ticket you blew off 25 years ago out of state, and the Bench Warrant that was issued on you as a result of your non-appearance. (Real example. I don't have to make this stuff up.) It has been waiting, all this time, and you had better get it settled before more trouble comes your way as others find out about it.

If that's not you, no problems, mate.

WHAT NOT TO DO

Don't be impatient. It is possible to contact the ATF and find out the status of your application. (No, I will not print the phone number.) What this means is, the agent you get on the phone has to stop doing whatever they are doing, go to the routing desk, find which examiner got your application, then go find them and get a rough estimate of where your application is, relative to the others and relative to where the examiner is in the stack of forms. In other words, you just put two people – the agent and the examiner – that much further behind in the work they were doing. Stop it. Stop it right now!

The dealer can only estimate, based on how long the wait was for the customer who picked up their suppressor earlier that week. He can call, if you insist, but he most likely has the same attitude about interrupting the agent and examiner that I just explained.

Dealers are also vague about how long it takes for a simple reason: it varies. Two applications can go in the mail the same day, and yet return, approved, six, seven, eight months later, a week or more apart.

TRUSTS

There was a time when trusts were en vogue. A trust (there are many types) is a legal entity that is viewed as a person, an entity which can own property, be it physical or intellectual. As far as the law is concerned, a trust is a person, one with limited rights (a trust can't vote, for example, or drive a car), but with others that are greater than those of a person.

For instance, an inheritable trust is one where you lock what you want to pass on into the trust, and it gets portioned out when you die. The list of property and the process are not a matter of public record (unlike a will, which is a matter of public record, filed at the county courthouse) and it cannot be contested. That's right, no probate on trusts. People can contest a trust, and when there is enough at stake, people do. But generally, as long as the person involved wasn't absolutely round-the-bend crazy, the trust will stand. The courts are loathe to overturn or change a trust, because doing so negates the whole point of a trust.

You'll still have to fill out a 4473 when you go to pick up your suppressor. You are, after all, picking up a firearm, so there's no escaping that.

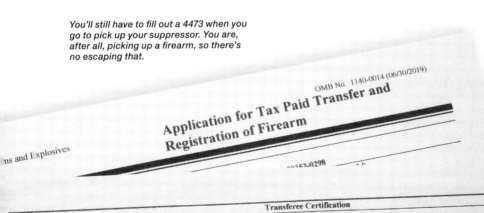

OMB No. 1140-0014 (06/30/2019)

Application for Tax Paid Transfer and Registration of Firearm

ns and Explosives

00152-0298

Transferee Certification

12. Law Enforcement Notification *(See instruction 2f)*

The transferee is to provide notification of the proposed acquisition and possession of the firearm described on this Form 4 by providing a c
completed form to the chief law enforcement officer in the agency identified below:

Name and Title of Official

Agency or Department Name

Address (Street address or P.O. Box, City, State and Zip Code) to which sent (mailed or delivered))

Information for the Chief Law Enforcement Officer

This form provides notification of the transferee's intent to acquire and possess a National Firearms Act (NFA) firearm. No action on your part is requir
have information that may disqualify this person from acquiring or possessing a firearm, please contact the NFA Branch at (304) 616-4500 or NFA@atf
items 14.a through 14.h or 16.b or 16.c could disqualify a person from acquiring or possessing a firearm. Also, ATF will not approve an application if
of the firearm is in violation of State or local law.

13. **Transferee Necessity Statement** *(See instruction 2e)*

, have a reasonable necessity to possess the machinegun, short-ba

The trust that involved NFA items was a bit different. Here, the trust owned the NFA items, be they machine guns, suppressors, etc., as an artificial person. You know, a non-voting, non-driving person. This did a couple of things, but it did not avoid the matter of the transfer tax.

As a "person" the trust still had to pay the $200 per transfer tax. No big deal. Since a "person" as the trust was the end-recipient, the government believes the tax has to be paid, and has insisted on it all along. This is different than your local NFA dealer receiving a suppressor for their inventory. Since the item is not yet in the possession of a person, nor has it been transferred to one, the dealer does not pay a tax on the suppressor that arrives at their door. You, the recipient, have that honor and duty.

The big deal of the NFA trust was this: the trust did not need a CLEO signature. Individuals, actual persons, had to have the CLEO signature, but trusts did not, and that made it possible to acquire suppressors where state law allowed it but the local CLEO refused to sign. Those who lived where suppressors were legal, but the local chief or sheriff would not sign, went to their attorneys and formed trusts, thus side-stepping the signature, and everyone was happy. (The smart ones went to their attorneys. It is possible to download the paperwork and legal boilerplate to form a trust on your own, but really? With suppressors at stake?)

Well, everyone was happy until a few people got sloppy. You see, a trust has to have members, called officers. Those people are either beneficiaries of or have access to the contents of the trust. For an inheritance, that would be beneficiaries. For an NFA trust, that would be officers. The deal was this, simply being an officer of a trust gave you access to the contents of the trust (the suppressors, SBRs, SBSs, machine guns, etc.), but it did not negate the restrictions on ownership or possession of firearms. If you were prohibited from owning (or handling) firearms, being an officer of a trust did not remove that restriction. You still were legally barred from possession. And yes, going to the range, being handed a firearm and shooting it was, for the purposes of the law, possession.

That meant the person forming the trust, who was the one paying for the items, had to be sure everyone listed on the trust, and brought as guests by officers, was lawful to own firearms.

Why was this a problem? The person forming the trust was responsible, and the officers could be listed or de-listed simply by being so-named by the person forming the trust. Once you formed a trust, you could put your family members, work buddies, etc., on the trust as officers, and they then had unsupervised access to the items in the trust. As the person who formed the trust, you could pull your suppressor/machine gun out of the safe, go to the range and shoot any time you wanted. If your brother was listed as an officer, he could drop by, and you could hand it to him and he'd be off to the range on his own.

Someone who was not an officer? You could not let them go alone. You could go to the range with them, and while there let them shoot the NFA firearm, but you had to be present. You also were responsible for knowing if they were able to lawfully possess a firearm.

An example: So, your son was okay, since you knew him and knew he was okay, so he's an officer of your NFA trust. Your daughter-in-law, having married him, was someone you knew, you hoped. Fine, she can be listed. And even if she isn't, your son can take her to the range, with the suppressors, as his guest. Her ne'r-do-well brother? The one with a DUI and domestic violence conviction? If your son and daughter-in-law took the brother to the range and let him handle and fire NFA weapons, that was a big no-no. A felony, in fact. What if the brother-in-law lied to you all and said he was clean, and you put him on the trust as an officer? Oops, a big no-no.

After a few occasions of such errors getting out into the press, there was a great outcry to "close the trust loophole." (Why is it everything that gets anti-gunners all worked up is a "loophole"?)

For a while it looked like the trust approach was going away entirely. Then, the ATF published their Rule 41F change to the NFA process.

In the Rule 41F change, individuals get a break; they no longer have to depend on the "kindness of strangers." You no longer need your CLEO to sign, you simply inform him/her that you are obtaining a suppressor. But, that change came at a cost.

Basically, every officer of an NFA trust had to be fingerprinted and go through a background check, not just the founder. That's right, before 41F the founder was fingerprinted and checked, and then he/she could just add anyone they wanted as an officer. Not smart, but we didn't set it up that way, now did we? Now, everyone has to be checked. But, there's a catch.

At the present time, it is a pretty cumbersome process, because each time a new item is added to the trust, everyone who is an officer has to get a background check again. How much of a hassle this is depends on your arrangements. If your trust is you and a few family members who all live in the same city, it isn't a big deal. You get fingerprinted, submit the paperwork and inform the CLEO. However, the more spread out your family or trust is, the more involved this becomes.

Let's say I personally have formed a trust and put my wife and my brothers and sisters on it. The six of us (me and my wife, two brothers, two sisters) live in five different cities. That means we'd have to travel to five different locations to get fingerprinted and have the paperwork for the background check. We'd have to inform five different CLEO's of the new item, and we'd have to wait until all six of us pass the background check before the trust got approval for the transfer.

If that works for you, then form a trust. If not, then don't. But it isn't the super-secret magical way to get a suppressor when you otherwise couldn't.

One other advantage of the trust is inheritance. When you die, what happens to your suppressors? Because by then you'll have more than one, trust me.

If you have a will, then the executor of your will has an interesting problem: they have the responsibility to handle your affairs and deal out your worldly goods. Or, you die and your wife inherits everything, because she's going to live longer.

The problem: you owned the suppressors, they did not. Absent an NFA trust, they cannot legally take possession of them until they have undergone the background check. We'll ignore for the moment the small detail of the transfer tax. How will they take possession of your property on the occasion of your death?

A trust solves that problem, provided they are listed as officers. Otherwise, your executor and your attorney will have to work fast, and depend on the kindness of the ATF and the local police to sit on your suppressors until they can get the heir or heirs approved for transfers.

MAKING A TRUST

As mentioned, not all trusts are the same. Also, state law differs in the details. You would be wise to go to an NFA-specific attorney who has handled NFA trusts before to have yours drawn up. The attorney who handled your home purchase, your insurance claim, or the probate of your late uncle's will are no-doubt all fine people. But if they have never worked on an NFA trust before, do you want to put your suppressors (and perhaps your freedom) at risk by having them handle this new thing?

Go to the experts. The dealer who sells you your suppressor probably has a list of NFA trust attorneys. If not, ask your attorney to find an NFA trust attorney. He or she will have the inside resources to track that person down.

CHAPTER 13

TRAVEL & PAPERWORK

• • •

You should have a copy of your Form 4 with you every time you leave the house with your suppressor. A copy. Do not take the original with you. If you made your suppressor instead of buying it – a lawful thing to do – keep a copy of the Form 1 that was approved.

Your approved Form 4, with its tax stamp affixed, is a tax document. It is also proof of lawful ownership. It is, to a certain extent, a piece of paper like your 1040 IRS form, and also like the title to the car you are driving. This form is too precious, too valuable, and not easily replaced, so you make sure you don't lose it. Make a copy of it and keep the copy with the suppressor.

Do the same thing for any SBR, SBS, etc., that you own, especially if it travels with the suppressor as a set.

Some people make reduced copies, some make a full-sized copy and fold it up like a firearms origami challenge. I've even seen people who traveled not just with the copy on paper, but a photograph of it on their phone.

I have a bunch of approved forms, and I made copies of each and laminated them in three-hole punched pages. I just take the binder with me, along with copies of my other essentials.

Here's the deal: this is a tax document. So it is in an in-between area. As proof of ownership, it is pretty definitive. Since there is no expiration date, it, like the title to your car, does not need to be renewed, period. (You renew the plate at the DMV, which plate is permission to drive on public roads, but you do not renew the title.)

So, you go to the range, and while you're unpacking your gear the Range Officer walks up and says, "I'll need to see a copy of your Form 4 to make sure your suppressor is legal." My initial reaction would be something rude, but not necessarily abusive. As far as I know, there is no legal basis for a range, gun club, etc., to see your suppressor paperwork to ensure that it is legal. You can argue, pointing out that they don't ask for proof of lawful ownership of the firearms on the line, but if that's the range policy, that's the range policy. Pack up and leave, and find someplace else to shoot.

What if he says, "We need to make a copy for our files, to make sure your suppressor is legal"? That gets a quick and firm "Bite me" from me, and packing up ensues, never to return to that place.

What about a police officer? You're at the range, no one there has ever seen a suppressor before (and that is a situation that will become increasingly rare, believe me), and he says, "I'm going to check with my supervisor to see if those are legal." Since the ATF approved your transfer, and they always (always!) defer to state law in such things, the mere fact that you have it and the Form 4 should be clear. However, he/she is going to check. "No problem, officer. I'll be right here once you are done checking." And say it sincerely, no attitude or other snark.

What if they want to see the Form 4? Show them the Form 4. Arguing with the police is a no-win situation. What if he/she wants to make a copy? Do not argue, but try to explain. "Officer, that is a tax document. The IRS doesn't like it when tax documents get copied unless they are in the investigation. If you don't mind, I'll just sit here quietly while you talk it over with your supervisor." It wouldn't hurt to have the phone number of the nearest ATF office with you. "Officer, this is the business card of the ATF agent I have talked to. A quick phone call should clear things up."

What are the chances that any of these will happen? Slim to none. Despite what the hand-wringing news media like to put on the evening news, the police don't usually just go around making trouble for everyone. If you are at the point where a police officer is interested in your suppressor (aside from "Hey, those are cool, how well does that one work?"), it's because you've screwed up someplace else in your life.

If you've just been pulled over for a DUI, that is not the time nor place to argue about the proper handling of paperwork on your suppressor. (And don't come running to the rest of us for sympathy over your plight, either.)

One more tip: if you do make a copy, make sure the serial number and model name are legible. Also, don't do anything cute like blacking out your name and address on the copy. If a police officer has a legitimate need to see your Form 4, he's also going to be asking for your driver's license. How is he/she going to make sure that the John Smith on the driver's license is also the John Smith on the Form 4, without an address? And, having an approved Form 4 without a name and address kinda defeats the purpose of having title to the suppressor, right?

Stop being a kid about it.

TRAVEL WITH SUPPRESSORS

There is a no-big-deal form, which you really don't need but some people insist on, for crossing state lines with NFA items. And there is a federal law which should provide you protection while traveling, but might not, and certainly won't in some places.

The form is the ATF Form 5320.20, also known as the "twenty form" or the "SBR form." This is a quickly-handled application in which you simply describe your SBR (or SBS, machine gun, or other NFA item) and the ATF does two things. They check to see that you and the item are both in the system, and that where you are going it is allowed.

If you are traveling to hunt or go to a class, and you are going, say, to Utah, then they check the boxes: Mr. Smith, okay. SBR, okay. Utah allows them, okay. Done. You want to vacation in Hawaii afterwards? "Mr. Smith, okay. SBR, okay. Hawaii? Not okay. Denied." You put down the timeframes, which can also be generous. If you want to visit your relatives in another SBR-friendly state, do not fill out an individual form each time you plan to go. Fill one out for 364 days, and

Yes, you should have paperwork with you. No, you do not travel with the originals. And no, you do not let someone take your copy.

name the state. Utah, January 1 through December 30. Done.

Here's the catch: you do not need to do this for the suppressor. Yes, it is an NFA item, but it is classified as a firearm. (That's what you checked on the 4473 form, remember?) If you do send it in, the examiner will take a quick look, mostly to see what state you are going to, and send it back approved or denied. And if denied, it will be because "You can't take it there, you should know that."

Considering how many states now allow ownership of suppressors, the denial list is pretty darned short. It is also all the usual suspects, so if you've done any looking at where guns are restricted, that's also the list of where you can't take your suppressor.

PROTECTION

The Firearm Owners Protection Act of 1986 was a big step forward during the Reagan Administration, but with a big bitter pill in it. The law did two things, one intended, and one rammed through at the literal last minute. What it was intended to do, and mostly does, is protect you while traveling. Basically, if you are in transit and your firearms are unloaded, locked up and inaccessible to you, you can drive through an otherwise prohibited area and the local law does not have purview.

Let us take as an example my travels some 25 years ago. The USPSA 3-Gun Nationals were held on Long Island, New York. (Don't ask, I never found out why there.) It was a long drive, and the short route was right through New York City. FOPA 86 should have, theoretically, protected me on that drive. Would it have? I have no way of knowing, since I was careful, followed all traffic laws, signs and signals, and never drew the attention of the authorities.

However, I also never stopped, not even for gas, food or the men's room. I most certainly could not have stopped overnight, with relatives or at a hotel. Again, theoretically, stopping for basic human needs like food, sleep or the bathroom, should, in a reasonable world, still have you under the protection of the law. To anyone who tries to put "reasonable" and "NYC gun laws" in the same sentence, and not be loudly laughed at, all I can say is be my guest.

FOPA 86 should offer protection while traveling. However, the basic attitude of the authorities in gun-unfriendly jurisdictions is, "So, sue us."

And some go further. There is an unfortunate (and exceedingly stupid) court precedent that greatly limits the protection FOPA 86 can provide. If you, for instance, happen to fly into NYC, and for whatever reason have to collect your luggage (even to get to a connecting flight), NYPD can arrest you, and has done so a number of times. How? Why? How, because you are in possession of an unregistered firearm in NYC. Why? You'll have to ask the people in charge. Oh, and here's the Catch 22: you aren't a resident of NYC, so there is no way you can register your firearm there.

If you are flying and your luggage gets transferred from one flight to another without you having to handle it, then you're probably okay. However, if you are arriving on an international flight, you have to collect your luggage before you can go through Customs and Immigration.

I have, a few times, been flying back to the U.S. from overseas, transporting firearms, and in the back of my mind hoping there's no emergency that causes the flight to be diverted to NYC or other such jurisdiction. It was bad enough flying through Canada, and I had permission to do that.

There are two ways to deal with such a geographic predicament, both simple. One, you drive around that state or city. That could be tough, considering the size of some states. Two, do what I did: behave yourself, make sure everything in your possession is absolutely legal, and simply don't draw the attention of the authorities.

This second approach might not work so well if you are, for instance, the victim of a traffic accident. Let's say you get t-boned, and even if you aren't hurt, the officer is going to look at the scattered ammo on the pavement and think, "There's something here I should pay attention to."

Or, you're injured and have to be taken to the hospital. The police will do an inventory of your vehicle before it is towed for one simple reason: the department requires it. The department does not want to be sued because "the attaché case with my lottery winnings was in the trunk, and someone took it." (You think I can make this stuff up?)

They will inventory your car before it is towed (the tow company doesn't want the liability exposure, either) and you will get back everything they found. Unless, of course, your AR-15, suppressor and hollowpoints are verboten in that state or city, in which case you will be arrested.

Before you start getting all paranoid, there aren't that many places where this is a problem. Most of them are places you won't want to go to anyway, and they can be identified and avoided.

HUGHES AMENDMENT

The Hughes Amendment was the last-minute addition to FOPA 86 that barred the future production of transferable machine guns. Those existing could be bought, sold, traded, etc., and new ones for law enforcement and the military could be manufactured. But no new ones could be made for general, commercial sale. That's how it came to be that I saw that $25,000 M16, and we now are hip-deep in suppressors.

SUMMARY

Make a copy of your Form 4. Keep it with your suppressor, and file the original away where it will be safe. Then, follow John Farnam's Rule: Don't go to stupid places, don't travel with stupid people, and don't do stupid things.

THREAD LISTS

. . .

The following thread patterns are common for various calibers and particular firearms.

ENGLISH

1/2-28	AR-15 and other .223/5.56 rifles and hand-guns, 9mm pistols, .22LR and other rimfires
1/2-36	9mm fixed-mount, carbines
.578-28	.45 ACP pistols
5/8-24	.308 and other .30 rifles (can be used on smaller-diameter bullet calibers)
7/16-24	.300 magnums
9/16-24	.300 magnums
3/4-24	.338 Lapua Magnum

METRIC

13.5Mx1 LH	European .45 pistols
14.5Mx1 LH	European .45 pistols
16Mx1 LH	European .45 pistols
18Mx1	.338 Lapua Magnum

SPECIALTIES

3-lug	HK MP5 mount

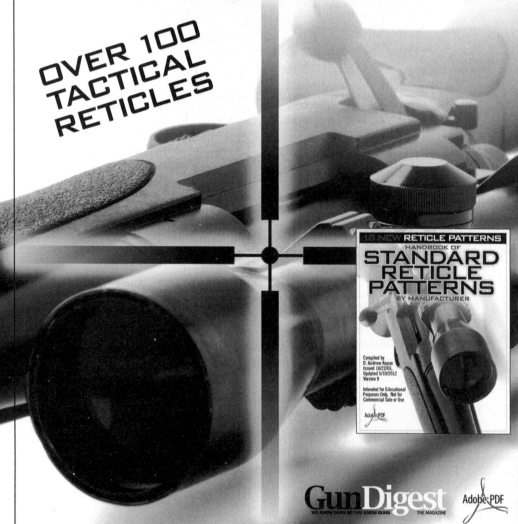